D0926865

TRANSLATING

THE

BIBLE

*Published to commemorate the 350th Anniversary
of the King James Version of the Holy Bible*

BY THE SAME AUTHOR

The Economic Background of the Gospels
New Horizons of the Christian Faith
The Growth of the Gospels
Form Criticism: A New Method of New Testament Research
The Beginnings of Our Religion
Frontiers of Christian Thinking
Can We Still Believe in Immortality?
The Idea of a Theological College
The Gospel of the Kingdom
The Practice of Religion
The Earliest Gospel
An Introduction to New Testament Thought
How to Read the Bible
Early Christianity: Collected Papers of Burton Scott Easton
    (*edited*)
The Gospels, Their Origin and Their Growth
Hellenistic Religions: The Age of Syncretism
Ancient Roman Religion
Ancient Judaism and the New Testament
Basic Christian Beliefs
Commentary on *Mark* in *The Interpreter's Bible*
Harper's Annotated Bible: *Matthew, Mark, John, Hebrews*
The Way of Peace
Christ's Victory and Ours
The Passion of the King
The Life and Times of Jesus
The Early Days of Christianity
Translation of Johannes Weiss, *Primitive Christianity*
Translation of Martin Dibelius, *The Message of Jesus Christ*
Translation of Martin Dibelius, *Jesus*
New edition of Edwin Hatch, *The Influence of Greek Ideas on*
    Christianity

The first Booke of Moses, called

in Hebrewe ᵃ Bereschith, and in
Greeke, ᵇ Genesis.

ᵃ That is, in the beginning.
ᵇ That is, generation, or creation.

The first Chapter.

1 HOw Heauen and earth, 3 the Light, 6 the Firmament, 16 the Sunne, the Moone, the Starres, 21 and fishes in the Sea, 24 and all beastes, and foules were made by the word of God, 26 and how man also was created.

Act. 14. 15.

Although the workes of God both in the creation, and in his spirituall operation in man, seeme rude and imperfect at the first: yet God by the working of his holy Spirit, bringeth all things to a perfection at the end.

b *The consideration of heauen & earth was imperfect and darke, and yet not vtterly dead: but that the power and strength of Gods Spirit, as it were, sate vpon it to make it liuely to continue vnto the worlds end.*
Hebr. 11. 3.
Pſal. 3. 2. 6.
The second day.
† Hebr. A stretching out, or setting abroad.
As the sea and riuers, from those waters that are aboue the firmament, which are separated by most pure, & they should be incorruptibile vnto the worlds end.
The thirde day.
Pſal. 1. 2. 7.
The fourth day.
Pſal. 36. 7.
Deut. 4. 19.
& 17. 3.
Christ is light vnto whome we serue, & whatsoeuer moueth vs, but our God, the tokens of his mercy, & so warth.

IN the beginning God created heauen and earth.

2 And the earth was ᵃ without forme, and was voyd: and darkenes was vpon the face of the deepe, and the ᵇ Spirit of God mooued vpon the face of the waters.

3 And God saide, * Let there be light : and there was light.

4 And God sawe the light that it was good : and God diuided the light from the darkenes.

5 And God called the light, Day, and the darkenesse, Night : and the euening and the morning were the first day.

6 * And God said, Let there be a † firmament betweene the waters and waters.

7 And God made the firmament, and set a diuision betweene the waters which were vnder the firmament, and the waters that were aboue the firmament : and it was so.

8 And God called the firmament, Heauen : and the euening and the morning were the second day.

9 And God said, * Let the waters vnder the heauen be gathered together into one place, and let the dry land appeare : and it was so.

10 And God called the dry land the earth, and the gathering together of waters called hee the Seas : and God saw that it was good.

11 And God saide, * Let the earth bring foorth bud and greene herbe apt to seede, and fruitfull trees, yeelding fruit after his kinde, which hath seed in it selfe vpon the earth : and it was so.

12 And the earth brought foorth greene herbe apt to seed after his kind, and tree yeelding fruit, which had seede in it selfe after his kinde.

13 And God sawe that it was good. And the euening and the morning were the thirde day.

14 And God said, Let there be * lights in the firmament of heauen, that they may diuide the day and the night, and let them bee * for ᵈ signes, and seasons, and for dayes, and yeeres.

15 And let them bee for lights in the firmament of the heauen, that they may giue light vpon the earth : and it was so.

16 And God made two great lightes : a great light to rule the day, and a lesse light to rule the night, and he made starres also.

17 And God set them in the firmament of the heauen, to shine vpon the earth,

18 And to rule the day and night, and to make difference betweene the light and the darkenes : and God saw that it was good.

19 And the euening and the morning were the fourth day.

20 And God said, * Let the waters bring forth mooving creature that hath life, and foule that may flie vpon the earth in the open firmament of heauen.

21 And God created great whales, and euery liuing and moouing creature, which the waters brought foorth after their kinde : and God sawe that it was good.

22 And God blessed them, saying, Bee fruitfull, and multiply, and fill the waters of the sea, and let foule multiply in the earth.

23 And the euening and the morning were the fifth day.

24 And God saide, Let the earth bring foorth liuing creature after his kinde, cattell, worme, and beastes of the earth after his kinde : and it was so.

25 God made the beast of the earth after his kinde, and cattel after his kinde, and euery thing that creepeth vpon the earth, after his kind : and God saw that it was good.

26 God saide, * Let vs make man in our Image, after our likenesse, and let them haue rule of the fish of the sea, and of the foule of the aire, and of cattell, and of all the earth, and of euery creeping thing that creepeth vpon the earth.

27 So God created man in his ʰ owne Image, in the Image of God created he him, male and female created he them.

28 And God blessed them, and God saide vnto them, Bee fruitfull, and multiply, and replenish the earth, and subdue it, and haue dominion of the fish of the Sea, and foule of the aire, and of euery liuing thing that moueth vpon the earth.

29 And God said, Beholde, I haue giuen you euery hearbe bearing seede, which is in the vpper face of all the earth, and euery tree, in the which is the fruite of a tree, bearing seede, that they may be meat vnto you :

30 To euery beast of the earth also, and to

The fift day.
4. Efd. 6. 74.
As fish and wormes: which sticke, swimme, or creepe.

f Blessing in Scripture signifieth abundance : that is, he gaue them fruitfulnesse by his word.

The sixth day.

Col. 3. 10.
g *Moses speaketh in the plurall number, signifying two persons to be in the Godhead, that the Father is the creation of mankinde hath his wisdom and Spirit.*
h *This Image and likenesse of God in man is expounded, where it is written, that man was created to be like God in righteousnesse and true holinesse, meaning by these words, all perfection, as immortalitie, wisedome, trueth, innocencie, power, &c.*

TRANSLATING THE BIBLE

BY FREDERICK C. GRANT

GREENWICH · CONNECTICUT · 1961

LIBRARY

APR 3 - 1961

UNIVERSITY OF THE PACIFIC

© *1961 by the Seabury Press, Incorporated*
Library of Congress Catalog Card Number: 61-5794
3-13-61
Design by Stefan Salter
Printed in the United States of America
344-1160-C-5   102168

BS
450
G76

TO THE RIGHT REVEREND

HORACE W. B. DONEGAN,

D.D., S.T.D., D.C.L.,

BISHOP OF NEW YORK,

with admiration and affection

Contents

FRONTISPIECE: *a page of the Bishops' Bible, in the Bodleian Library, Oxford, showing marginal revisions and alterations which correspond closely with the King James text as printed in 1611. (See pp. 77-78.)*

TRANSLATING

THE

BIBLE

I.

THE

HEBREW

BIBLE

THE BIBLE is the most translated book in the world! No other writing, or collection of writings, either sacred or secular, has been translated so often, or into so many languages and dialects. When the American Bible Society produced, in 1938, its admirable *Book of a Thousand Tongues*, edited by Dr. Eric North, the title was a correct description of the Bible. Now the number is over eleven hundred—1151 Bibles or parts of Bibles.

The translation of Holy Scripture into languages spoken where Christian missionaries are at work is an obviously practical step, often with consequences reaching far beyond the conversion and edification of a group of new Christians who know only their own tongue. Repeatedly in the history of Europe and the Near East, the translation of the Bible or of some parts thereof, e.g., the gospels, has been the beginning and foundation of a national literature. There is a Scottish missionary in the high Andes, whose forty years' ministry has been devoted to the descendants of the ancient Incas, living at an altitude of two miles or more. Into their language he has translated parts of the Bible. Like the ancient Anglo-Saxon gospels among the English, his translation of Mark was printed in large letters, like a children's book; it was the first book of any kind that these people had ever seen. Another missionary, an American, has worked for years among a tribe in the interior of Africa. His vocabulary and grammar were the first textbooks of their language; his translation of parts of the Bible was at first their only literature. Now he has added the traditional "oral literature" of the tribe, their accounts of creation and early history, their wars and migrations, their folk-tales, songs, and proverbs. A translation of the Bible, or of a part of it, was thus the beginning of their literature.

The same is true of many other areas. The debt of later English literature to sixteenth and seventeenth century Bible translations, especially the King James Version, and of later German literature to Luther's German Bible, is generally acknowledged. Centuries earlier, similar results had followed the Gothic and Armenian translations, the ancient Coptic and Syriac. There were, of course, exceptions to this rule. Latin was already known in both Africa and Gaul long before the Old Latin version of the Bible began to appear, and certainly Ptolemaic Greek was well known in Egypt before the Septuagint was produced. Aramaic language and literature existed before the Old Testament Targum. But these exceptions are due to the fact that the Bible originated in the midst of a civilization—really of two civilizations, the Hebrew and the Graeco-Roman. It was its further dissemination which has produced something novel and creative in the intellectual history of the human race. In a quite secular and everyday sense as well as in the sacred sense of revelation, the translation and circulation of Holy Scripture was the sowing of the seed of a new life of intelligence, imagination, learning, poetry, art. "The sower sows the word" (Mark 4:14).

In this long story, from the very beginning of the Bible as a written book or collection of books, the sacred text has been translated into many different languages and dialects. And, as we shall see, almost from the beginning there have been "authorized versions," with later revisions or editions, resulting in "revised versions"—and even in "revised standard versions," from time to time. The story of Bible translation is almost as long as the story of the Bible itself; its translation into other tongues began even before the sacred text itself was complete.

It would be a mistake to assume that only one motive led to the translation of the Bible, for example the missionary motive (just described), or the educational or the literary—though these latter motives were strongly present throughout the early centuries and also in the Middle Ages, as well as in modern times when missionary and educational aims often combine or coincide. But the purely literary motive, as in the tale of Ptolemy's authorization of the Septuagint,[1] is quite subsidiary and really unimportant. The demand for an accurate translation of a sacred text viewed as divine Law, or as the formulation of a body of divinely revealed truth, i.e., as the basis of a theological system—this was still another motive, one which came to its height in

[1] See Chapter II.

late medieval Scholasticism and in early Protestantism. Reformers who envisaged a political state or a civil society ruled by divine Law insisted upon a precise and literal translation of the sacred books in which this code was set forth. (A modern parallel may be seen in the new Turkish translation of the Koran issued during the political reforms of 1925.) Even controversy led to the demand for more accurate texts: controversy, theological or ecclesiastical, which was often bitter and relentless, and sometimes resulted in violence, or even in judicial murder. But even so—as St. Paul said of unworthy preachers—"Christ was proclaimed" (Phil. 1:15-18); the Bible was translated, circulated, and studied.

The motives leading to Bible translation thus have deep sociological and psychological origins. Eduard Meyer began his classic History of Antiquity (*Geschichte des Altertums*) with a survey of Anthropology, which in his definition included both the external social conditions and the inner realm of thought and language of early mankind. In 1884 this seemed fantastic and revolutionary—though he had good precedents, Thucydides and the Old Testament; in 1907, when his second edition was ready, the principle was almost a commonplace among historians, for the revolution had taken place in the writing of history; today, no one questions it. It is recognizable even in the history of Bible translation. Ezra "the priest, the scribe," insisted upon the Torah being well understood, i.e., both translated and expounded, for he intended to make it the law of the newly refounded Jewish State, the Second Commonwealth. (Law was the ruling conception of ancient Judaism as restored or refounded by Ezra—but by no means its only conception.) For the medieval Schoolmen likewise—St. Thomas

Aquinas, for example—the Gospel was the *nova lex*, the "new law." John Wycliffe urged his associates to proceed with the English translation and dissemination of the Scriptures, because in them the true law of the state was contained. Less than two centuries later, merchants in the City of London subsidized William Tyndale's New Testament, relying upon it to bring about ecclesiastical reforms which they hoped to see. Even in the present English Coronation Service, a copy of the Bible is handed to the new sovereign with the admonition to live and rule by the Scriptures. "Here is wisdom: This is the royal Law: These are the lively Oracles of God."

It may of course be said that the view of the Scriptures as *law* (primarily moral law, but also including canon law, especially polity, i.e., rules for the organization and administration of the church) is a medieval inheritance, or, older still, an ancient Roman; and that the view of Scripture as *theology* is specifically Greek (patristic) and Scholastic, i.e., derived from the ancient church fathers and the medieval theologians; the view of the Scriptures as a source for *liturgical* material is really pre-Christian, and goes back to the ancient Jewish synagogue. But all these views are the consequence of certain special emphases, resulting from social or even political conditions and interests. The origin of all three views goes back a long way, even (a) to Ezra's inauguration of the reading and interpretation of the Law as the binding authority within the new Jewish Commonwealth, and (b) to the constant and closely detailed study of the Scriptures in the ancient synagogue, which soon supplemented the Torah with the other books in the Hebrew Bible.

It was one of the most dramatic and most significant

events in religious history when Ezra "the priest, the scribe," arrived in Jerusalem in the year 397 B.C. and confronted his countrymen with the written Torah (Law) which was henceforth to govern the life of the new Jewish Commonwealth. Forty-seven years earlier, in 444 B.C., the Jewish Governor, Nehemiah, had arrived and begun the restoration of the city's walls. Seventy-six years earlier still, in 520 B.C., the prophets Haggai and Zechariah had tried to revive the broken spirits of the scattered survivors of the ancient Hebrew state, living miserably in or near the ruins of their sacred capital which had been captured by the Babylonians in 597 B.C. and totally destroyed in 586. The long "seventy years" of the Exile—seventy-one years, from the fall of Jerusalem in 586 to the restoration of the temple in 515— was a period of depression and dismay for the survivors in Palestine. But in far-away Babylonia the study and codification, the copying and interpretation of the sacred Law had steadily continued; so that when the time came for Ezra to launch his reform movement, and to place the new colony upon a firm foundation, the Torah had probably reached about the form in which it is still read in our Bible, viz., the Pentateuch, the first five books of the Old Testament. The story of Ezra's reinauguration of the Law is told in Nehemiah 7:73b—8:8.

> And when the seventh month had come, the children of Israel were in their towns. And all the people gathered as one man into the square before the Water Gate; and they told Ezra the scribe to bring the book of the law of Moses which the Lord had given to Israel. And Ezra the priest brought the law before the assembly, both men and women and all who could hear with understanding, on the first day

of the seventh month. And he read from it facing the square before the Water Gate from early morning until midday, in the presence of the men and the women and those who could understand; and the ears of all the people were attentive to the book of the law. And Ezra the scribe stood on a wooden pulpit which they had made for the purpose; and beside him stood Mattithiah, Shema, Anaiah, Uriah, Hilkiah, and Maaseiah on his right hand; and Pedaiah, Mishael, Malchijah, Hashum, Hashbaddanah, Zechariah, and Meshullam on his left hand. And Ezra opened the book in the sight of all the people, for he was above all the people; and when he opened it all the people stood. And Ezra blessed the Lord, the great God; and all the people answered, "Amen, Amen," lifting up their hands; and they bowed their heads and worshiped the Lord with their faces to the ground. Also Jeshua, Bani, Sherebiah, Jamin, Akkub, Shabbethai, Hodiah, Maaseiah, Kelita, Azariah, Jozabad, Hanan, Pelaiah, the Levites, helped the people to understand the law, while the people remained in their places. And they read from the book, from the law of God, clearly [or with interpretation]; and they gave the sense, so that the people understood the reading.

The scene is unforgettable. Its consequences reached far into the future, even to the present day, for Judaism was henceforth "the religion of the Book." The adoption of the Law by the assembled people is told in what follows. It reminds us of the adoption of the Law by the Israelites at Sinai in the time of Moses: "All that the Lord has spoken we will do" (Exod. 19:8). The narrative is traditional, and combines various sources, chiefly the memoirs of Nehemiah and Ezra. Parts of Ezra are not in Hebrew but Aramaic (4:8—6:18; 7:12-26; so also is Dan. 2:4b—7:28; and so are the two verses in Gen. 31:47 and Jer. 10:11). In the case of Ezra-Nehemiah it would seem that a fragmentary work, either a Hebrew book which had been translated into Aramaic, or an Aramaic book which had been translated into Hebrew, had to be pieced-out from the translation.[2] But behind this fragmentary and re-edited record the course of events seems clear. Ezra's reform was designed to carry out the program which the prophets had suggested. Israel's political catastrophes had been the consequence of national sin and disobedience. To insure the future survival and stability of the Jewish people, it was necessary to make sure of their complete obedience to the revealed will of God set forth in the Torah. Hence the reading, study, interpretation, and observance of the Law was the first duty of all Jews. There was a precedent for this from the days before the Exile (Deut. 31:10-13), but the custom had not begun early enough.

All through the Feast of Booths, Ezra read to the assembly "the book of the law of God" (Neh. 8:18), and on the twenty-fourth day they read again (9:3). The interpreters who assisted in the reading and made clear its meaning are thought to have been translators who turned the traditional Hebrew of the Pentateuch into the current Aramaic. This was still the language of the common people of Palestine—and of other peoples in Western Asia—and it was to be their language for many centuries to come. These "assistants" were the forerunners of the methurgemans (translators) in the early synagogue and also of the

[2] There is a certain appropriateness in the use of Aramaic in these sections, which contain official documents and reflect the common language of the Neo-Babylonian and Persian Empires.

scribes who copied and explained the Law in New Testament times. In the ancient world, to "interpret" meant both to translate and to expound.

It was out of this at first oral translation of the Torah that the old Palestinian Targum developed, fragments of which have been found in the Cairo Geniza. This Targum was eventually—several centuries later—superseded by the Targum of Onkelos on the Pentateuch and that of Jonathan on the Prophets, which were brought to Palestine from Babylonia; but these later translations were in literary Aramaic, which was the official language of the Near East and also of Talmudic scholarship. (Even long after the Greek conquest of the Near East, Aramaic continued in general use.) A complete copy of the Old Palestinian Targum of the Pentateuch, in 450 parchment folios, has recently been discovered in the Vatican Library by Professor A. Diez Macho of Barcelona University; and so at last the long-lost work will soon be available to scholars. This is the Targum, the Aramaic translation of the Torah, which was known and used by Jesus and his disciples in the synagogues of Palestine in the first century, perhaps used also by the evangelist Matthew, and probably by the historian Josephus. It is quite probable, as Professor Paul Kahle observes, that this old Targum never received a fixed form, but was frequently revised and altered into closer conformity with the Hebrew original. But its existence and use supports the statement that the Bible has been *translated* ever since its beginning as a sacred collection.

The reader may have observed the frequent references to the Targum in the marginal readings of the Revised Standard Version (RSV) of the Old Testament, where it is often cited along with the Greek translation, or with the Syriac, the Old Latin, or those Hebrew manuscripts which were found among the Dead Sea Scrolls. To take the text of one book only, that of the prophet Isaiah, the following verses contain interesting examples of such citations of evidence:

Greek: Isa. 6:2, 12, 16; 3:13; 5:17; 9:20; 10:34; 16:10; 17:9; 26:7; 38:17; 47:13; 48:11; 65:7; 66:2 + Syriac.

Aramaic Targum: 14:19; 26:9; 27:8; 44:4; 50:11 + Syriac; 51:16; 52:14; 56:12; 64:7 + Syriac and Old Latin; 66:18.

Dead Sea Scroll "Isaiah A," here cited as "one ancient Ms.": 3:24; 14:4, 30; 15:9; 21:8; 23:2; 33:8; 45:2, 8; 49:14; 51:19; 53:10 + Latin; 60:19; 64:7 + Latin.

But the RSV has followed no one authority slavishly, either the traditional Hebrew (the "Masoretic" text as established and vocalized by the Masoretes between the sixth and ninth centuries after Christ) or the Greek, the Old Latin, or the Syriac, or even the Aramaic Targum. In no case has the RSV adopted a reading found *only* in the Targum.

No scholar in our century has done more to establish the text of the Old Testament or to recover its earliest form than Professor Paul Kahle of Bonn University, now living in Oxford. His researches into the whole realm of early manuscripts and versions have pushed back the frontiers of Old Testament textual research by several centuries. His edition of Rudolf Kittel's *Biblia Hebraica* marked an important step forward in the publication of the Hebrew text of the Old Testament. Fortunately for the RSV translators, this edition appeared just before they set about their task in 1937. And it is quite clear from Kahle's work, and from his words, that no one form of text, or version, can be taken as final. In all textual research, short of a fortunate discovery of the autograph, results are never more than an approximation to the original, and the best results we can hope for are the closest possible approximation. No manuscript or version is infallible.

For example, the American Translation (the University of Chicago *Complete Bible*, 1935) is supported by the Old Palestinian Targum in its rendering of Exodus 22:5f. Both verses are made to refer to damage caused by a neighbor burning over his field and letting the fire get out of control. The RSV, on the other hand, has rendered the Hebrew text:

> When a man causes a field or vineyard to be grazed over, or lets his beast loose and it feeds in another man's field, he shall make restitution from the best in his own field and in his own vineyard. When fire breaks out and catches in thorns so that the stacked grain or the standing grain or the field is consumed, he that kindled the fire shall make full restitution.

Here probability surely supports the traditional text. (1) The Targum makes v.6 repeat, in effect, the regulation set forth in v.5. (2) Ancient law generally recognized the claim for damages done to property by loose cattle and by uncontrolled fire. In the ancient Roman code, *The Twelve Tables*, for example, the laws appear in similar form and in the same order as in the Old Testament (see VIII. 7, 10). The *actio de pastu pecoris* is followed by the *actio* covering damages done by careless opening of water courses which thus injure a neighbor's fields, and this in turn by damages due to irresponsible—or accidental—setting of fires.[3]

But *taken in combination* with other ancient versions, as we have seen, or with a form of Hebrew text older than the Masoretic (e.g., one found in the Cairo Geniza or among the Dead Sea Scrolls), the Aramaic Targum, either in one of its Old Palestinian forms or even in the later Babylonian (Onkelos and Jonathan), deserves most serious attention.

It is clearly evident that the Hebrew Bible, our Old Testament, has been translated almost from the beginning of its collection into a canon. Ezra's arrival at Jerusalem and his promulgation of the sacred Torah as the divine Law to govern the newly restored community marked the beginning of the collection and "canonization" of Scripture. A century later the "Prophets" were added, i.e., the historical and prophetic writings. By the middle of the second century B.C. all three parts of the Hebrew Bible were recognized. For when Sirach's grandson went down to Egypt and there made a translation of his grandfather's book of wisdom, our Ecclesiasticus, he referred to "the law and the prophets and the others that followed them," or to "the law, the prophecies, and the rest of the books." His interesting Prologue throws light not only upon the growth of the Old Testament but also upon the problems of translation, both ancient and modern.

> Whereas many great teachings have been given to us through the law and the prophets and the others that followed them, on account of which we should praise Israel for

[3] See Max Kaser, *Das römische Privatrecht,* I (Munich, 1955), p. 143f.

instruction and wisdom; and since it is necessary not only that the readers themselves should acquire understanding but also that those who love learning should be able to help the outsiders by both speaking and writing, my grandfather Jesus [Sirach], after devoting himself especially to the reading of the law and the prophets and the other books of our fathers, and after acquiring considerable proficiency in them, was himself also led to write something pertaining to instruction and wisdom, in order that, by becoming conversant with this also, those who love learning should make even greater progress in living according to the law.

You are urged therefore to read with good will and attention, and to be indulgent in cases where, despite our diligent labor in translating, we may seem to have rendered some phrases imperfectly. For what was originally expressed in Hebrew does not have exactly the same sense when translated into another language. Not only this work, but even the law itself, the prophecies, and the rest of the books differ not a little as originally expressed.

When I came to Egypt in the thirty-eighth year of the reign of Euergetes [132 B.C.] and stayed for some time, I found opportunity for no little instruction [or a copy affording no little instruction]. It seemed highly necessary that I should myself devote some pains and labor to the translation of the following book, using in that period of time great watchfulness and skill in order to complete and publish the book for those living abroad who wished to gain learning, being prepared in character to live according to the law.

It is clearly evident that from the very beginning the chief motive which led to the translation of Scripture has been the education and edification of the religious community, the congregation. From the outset, the Bible has been the book read at synagogue or church. It was also used in private study and devout meditation; but it was so used because *first of all* it was the book of the church, the congregation. Theologians and historians of religious thought sometimes appear to assume that the Bible has existed— has come into existence and has been handed down through the centuries—in a vacuum, and may therefore be interpreted without reference to the "believing congregation." But its initial place as well as its continuing place of honor is on the lectern, where it is read to the assembled people —as it was by Ezra and his assistants, and has been ever since. The ancient Haftarahs and Parashas (the passages selected for reading in the synagogue services) were followed in the Christian church by the "Lessons" or lections read at public worship. It is because of this *use* of the Bible that it was copied and recopied countless times, carefully preserved and handed on to posterity, in spite of persecution and destruction of both synagogue and church.

Bible translation has been, as a rule, at first oral, "in many parts and in different manners"; but in time the translations have been checked and rechecked, revised and re-revised, and brought into closer conformity with the original. Thus a great variety of translations have appeared—as we shall see—literal, paraphrastic, homiletical, doctrinal. For to translate has always meant to interpret, and the best translation has not always been the most literal. There are some modern "free" translations that really bring the reader into closer *rapport* with the ancient authors than any formal or "authorized" version. And yet the fact remains, clear and indisputable, that the most natural setting for the Bible is liturgical. It is the church's book, read aloud and devoutly heard "in the great congregation," the assembly of the people of God, gathered for the purpose of offering him their worship and of "hearing words from him." As we shall see, nowhere is this principle more true or more important than in the history of the English Bible. But it has always been true from the very beginning of the writing, reading, translating, and expounding of the Holy Scriptures.

This principle of *lectionary use*, involving the choice of books suitable for reading at public worship, was probably the most decisive factor in the formation of the church's biblical canon. Those books, and those alone, were admitted to the canon, the "approved list," which had already proved their suitability for such use, were uncontaminated by false teaching (for example, Gnostic doctrines), and were either derived from the sacred collection of the synagogue or were clearly "apostolic" in origin, authorship, and teaching.

II.

THE

GREEK

BIBLE

THE ancient maxim, *Ex Oriente lux*, "Out of the East comes light," has been strikingly exemplified in modern times. Out of a dark, dusty, windowless, airless store-chamber ("Geniza") in a long-abandoned synagogue in Old Cairo have come many manuscripts, and tens of thousands of fragments of manuscripts, of ancient Hebrew books. The "Damascus Document" (formerly called the "Zadokite Fragments") now recognised as closely related to the Manual of Discipline among the Dead Sea Scrolls; the long-lost Hebrew original of Sirach (Ecclesiasticus); many ancient liturgical books; copies, and fragments of copies, of the Sacred Scriptures—these were examined, classified, and finally, in 1896-98, removed to the library of Cambridge University by Dr. Solomon Schechter (he was later the President of the Jewish Theological Seminary, New York City). These fragments filled 164 boxes, and many of them have not even yet been deciphered or edited.

In 1945 came the news of another great find: a whole library of Gnostic books written in Coptic, buried centuries ago in a jar in a field near Nag Hammadi, south of Cairo. These also are still being studied, copied, edited and translated, and it may be several years before they are fully available to the world's scholars. It is the first large-scale collection of firsthand sources for one of the most important movements in early Christian history. There have been other important discoveries of manuscripts, in Egypt and elsewhere, for example the valuable Manichean fragments found at Turfan, written in Persian and Turkish and even in Chinese, and the various papyrus books discovered in the Fayûm.

In 1947 still another immensely valuable discovery was made, the so-called Dead Sea Scrolls, found in caves at Qumrân at the north-west corner of the Dead Sea, where they had been hidden away for safekeeping in large sealed jars, probably about A.D. 70. It is thought that this ancient library once belonged to an ascetic group, possibly Essenes, whose community disappeared at the time of the capture of Jerusalem by the Romans; before they left Qumrân they had buried their books, hoping some day to return. But like the servant who guarded the master of Minster Lovell, near Oxford, like those patriots who buried the Avignon tapestries, like many another who meant to return, the Qumrân ascetics never got back. And so for almost nineteen centuries their library has lain secretly hid in the rocky caves above the Dead Sea. It is probable that many of the books have been removed at various times by Bedouins who viewed them as curiosities, or by the ninth-century Karaites, who recognised their value; but enough remain to fill out in some measure our present-day knowledge of the Bible text and its translation and exposition during the final centuries before the rise of Christianity.

One of the most extraordinary features of this collection is the presence of fragmentary manuscripts of the *Greek translation* of the Old Testament, and of Hebrew manuscripts which agree in some ways more closely with that ancient translation than with the later standard Hebrew text; though on the whole the later Hebrew text is strongly attested by the Qumrân documents, and the most recently discovered manuscripts are most like it in form. For centuries it has been believed—correctly—that the Greek Old Testament was translated in Egypt, the oldest account of its origin being contained in the so-called *Letter of Aristeas.* This apocryphal letter dates from circa 100 B.C., but was ostensibly addressed to Philocrates in the reign of Ptolemy Philadelphus (285-246 B.C.) when the author represents the translation as being made. The story is that King Ptolemy heard about the excellent Jewish scriptures and insisted upon having a copy in Greek, for the great library he was collecting in Alexandria. So he sent an embassy, including the author, Aristeas, loaded with presents for the high priest in Jerusalem and conveying a request for a copy of the sacred books and for translators. The high priest agreed, and appointed six scholars from each of the twelve tribes—72 men in all—with a superb copy of the Law, written in letters of gold. Ptolemy received them gladly, and gave them a banquet at which, in good Greek and Oriental style, they conducted a symposium and displayed their learning. Following this public welcome they set about their proper task and began the translation of the Pentateuch. The King assigned them quarters on the Island of Pharos, just off the Delta, famous in ancient times for its lighthouse which could be seen for twenty miles at sea.

[Here] they met daily in a place which was pleasant for its quiet and its brightness [clear light?], and applied themselves to the task before them. And it so happened that the translation was completed in seventy-two days, just as if this had been arranged on purpose. [When the work was finished it was read to the Jewish community, who assembled at the place where the translation had been made. They praised it warmly and urged that copies should be made.]

After the books had been read, the priests and the elders among the translators and members of the Jewish community and the leaders of the people stood up and said that since the translation had been done so excellently and piously and in every way accurately, it was only proper that it should remain as it was and that no alteration should be made in it. And when the whole company expressed their approval, they bade them pronounce a curse, in accordance with their custom, upon anyone who should make any alteration [in it], either by adding anything, or by changing, in any way whatsoever, any of the words which had been written, or by making any omission. This was a very wise precaution, designed to insure that the book would be preserved without change for all time to come.

This apocryphal letter, a typical piece of propaganda, was designed, as Dr. Kahle and others think, to win support for one particular Greek version of the Torah by representing it as old, official, and authorized—fully authorized, in fact, by the Greek king, the Jewish high priest in Jerusalem, the seventy (-two) themselves, and the whole Jewish community in Alexandria! As Kahle points out, no one invents propaganda for what is already generally accepted. And the author of the epistle himself refers (§ 314) to "earlier and somewhat unreliable translations of the Law" (and see § 30). In fact, the earlier translations were viewed as sacred, and he tells the story of Theopompus, who went temporarily insane after trying to work into his secular history some of the incidents recorded in the "sacred and divine" writings; also a story of a tragic poet, Theodectes, who went temporarily blind after trying to include biblical incidents in a secular poem. Nevertheless, as often in legends, there are a few essential points of unquestioned veracity: the place, the general period, and the relation of the translation to the Jewish community.

Hebrew was little understood by the Jews at Alexandria, by this time (circa 100 B.C.), and Greek was used even in the synagogues. The new version—or revision—of the Law received the full approval of the whole Jewish community (the Jews then numbered two-fifths of the population of the city), and they wished it to take the place of all earlier translations. In this respect, the version evidently succeeded, and the Christians eventually took it over as *the* Greek translation, some of them viewing it as inspired (St. Irenaeus and St. Augustine, for example, so viewed it). How could they have done otherwise, since they accepted the story in the *Letter of Aristeas* as plain and simple truth? Incidentally, Aristeas uses the term "the Bible" for the first time (§ 316): *hē biblos*, meaning a collection of books (see also Sirach 24:23, where the books of the Pentateuch are "the" book, singular; 1 Macc. 1:56, 57; 12:9; 2 Macc. 8:23). He also uses the term "the scripture"

(§ 168 *hē graphē*). It was this "biblos," the Bible, to which in time were added authorized (i.e., officially approved and accepted) translations of the rest of the Old Testament books, and which thus eventually became "the Bible" of the early Christians. As soon as the church crossed the borders of Palestine, in its westward expansion, it became Greek-speaking everywhere for at least a hundred years, and in some areas has so remained ever since. As an inspired translation, the church made the Septuagint (i.e., done by the "Seventy" = LXX) the basis of further translations into languages in both East and West, and also North and South. The story in Aristeas was further elaborated, and made to include the whole Old Testament, miraculously translated by seventy men (or seventy-two) in seventy days, the translators working in pairs and discovering, day by day, that their translations agreed *literatim et verbatim*.

The Greek translation of the Old Testament was thus the creation, the possession, and really the lawful property of the Jewish Synagogue. As Christians made even greater use of it, after the breach between the synagogue and the church late in the first century, and turned its inspired locutions against the Jews themselves, the latter began providing themselves with more literal translations. Isaiah 7:14 was a case in point. The Septuagint read, "The (*or* A) virgin (*parthenos*) shall conceive and bear a son." But the Hebrew said only "a young woman" (*almah*), and this was scarcely a prediction of the Virgin Birth of Christ. So a Jewish translation was provided in which there could be no ambiguity: the Greek word chosen was *neanis*, "young woman," "girl," "maiden." The translation in which this expression was used was the famous one by Aquila, who is said to have been the emperor Hadrian's cousin, and to have superintended the rebuilding of Jerusalem as Aelia Capitolina after its destruction in A.D. 135. The version was hopelessly literal. Aquila even tried to translate (by the Greek word *syn* = "with") the particle *ēth*, which is only a sign used to indicate that the following noun is in the accusative case. Thus, in Genesis 1:1, he read, "God created with the heavens and with the earth"—which makes sense only if you know Hebrew and also know what Aquila was trying to do! But the day was at hand when Jewish scholars were to lay the utmost emphasis upon the "letter" of Scripture, and its *letters*, counting them, finding mystical reasons for their varying size, and recording every peculiar detail which they discovered in the manuscripts.

Another translator was Theodotion, who also lived, presumably, in the second century. What he undertook was not a new translation but a revision of the current Greek version into closer agreement with the current Hebrew text. He added some passages which the Septuagint had omitted, and provided a text which is often reflected in the New Testament quotations. That is, the text on which he worked may not have been the traditional Septuagint at all, but a Greek version also used by some of the New Testament writers. His version of Daniel was adopted by the church in preference to that of the "Seventy," and to this day it is the version included in the common text of the Greek Old Testament.

Finally, towards the end of the second century, a version was made by a Christian, an Ebionite named Symmachus. At least, this is the tradition about him. His version was known to Origen and was used by St. Jerome, who said that Symmachus "gave the sense of the scripture, not its literal language, as Aquila did."

Now with so many translations and revisions in use, all of which influenced one another, it became a question which of them was the original "Septuagint," i.e., the true, the inspired translation. And so, at the beginning of the third century, Origen of Alexandria (A.D. 186-253), the greatest biblical scholar of his time, set about a restoration of the true text of the Old Testament. His work resulted in the famous *Hexapla* ("six-fold"), in which he gave, in parallel columns, (1) the current Hebrew text—virtually identical with the later Masoretic; (2) this Hebrew text transliterated in Greek letters, thus giving the proper pronounciation of the unpointed (vowel-less) Hebrew—the vowels were added later by the Masoretes; (3) Aquila's Greek translation, the closest to the Hebrew in form; (4) the translation of Symmachus; (5) the Septuagint, revised by Origen himself; (6) the version of Theodotion, at the farthest remove from the original. In addition, Origen added, for the Book of Psalms, three additional versions, which were presumably anonymous, for they bear only the numbers of the columns: *Quinta, Sexta,* and *Septima* (or their equivalent in Greek). This vast encyclopedic "harmony of versions" must have run to 6500 pages, at least, and only parts of it were ever copied—e.g., a *Tetrapla,* giving Aquila, Symmachus, the Septuagint, and Theodotion. The original work was the prized treasure of the great Christian library at Caesarea in Palestine, where Jerome consulted it at the end of the fourth century, and where it remained until the library was destroyed during the Muslim conquest of Palestine in the seventh century. Except for the fifth column, Origen's revision of the Septuagint, only fragments survive. Cardinal Mercati, in 1896, found a fifth-century palimpsest fragment in the Ambrosian library at Milan (eleven Psalms in five of Origen's six columns).

Origen was a careful scholar and his revision of the Septuagint showed clearly, by the use of appropriate editorial symbols, whatever he had added to, omitted from, or altered in the traditional text. His purpose was to provide a version conforming as accurately as possible to the Hebrew text. Unfortunately, copyists who used Origen's Septuagint column as their model soon omitted these editorial symbols, with the result that what passed for the original Septuagint was only a private recension of it, some of it based on Theodotion (from which Origen freely borrowed). But fortunately, on the other hand, in the year 617, shortly before the destruction of the Caesarean library, Bishop Paul of Tella in Mesopotamia translated Origen's Septuagint column into Syriac, retaining all the editorial symbols. An eighth-century copy of this version still exists in the Ambrosian Library at Milan. It contains the Prophets, Job, Psalms, Proverbs, Ecclesiastes, and the Song of Solomon. There are also some fragments in the British Museum. Most of the rest of Origen's Hexapla has completely disappeared, though fragments are found here and there, and others may be hoped for—if more Genizas are discovered.

There are later revisions of the Septuagint, such as those by Eusebius of Caesarea, the church historian, by Hesychius, and by Lucian—the two latter were martyred in A.D. 311.

The task of editing and restoring the original of the Septuagint is one of the most complicated and difficult in the whole realm of biblical science. But it is under way! The great editions at Cambridge and Göttingen, the provisional editions of H. B. Swete and Alfred Rahlfs, the vastly erudite investigations of Paul Kahle and his school, the famous Bonn Seminar, the patient collation of scores of manuscripts in various parts of the world, all these contribute toward the common cause. It begins to appear that there probably never was a single "Septuagint" text, but a whole series of Greek translations, revisions, modifications and amplifications, which ought to be called, not "the" Septuagint but rather "the Greek translation," or, as Sir Frederic Kenyon used the term, "the Greek Bible."

The great manuscripts of the Greek Bible, which also include the early Christian writings, the New Testament, are well known: the fourth-century Codex Vaticanus, now in the Vatican Library at Rome, the best of all Greek Old and New Testament manuscripts; the fourth-century Codex Sinaiticus, discovered by Constantine Tischendorf in 1844 in the Monastery of St. Catherine on Mount Sinai, and now in the British Museum; the fifth-century Codex Alexandrinus, presented in 1628 to King Charles I by Cyril Lucar, the Greek Patriarch of Constantinople, and now in the British Museum; the fifth-century Codex Ephraemi (*rescriptus*, i.e., a palimpsest), now in the Bibliothèque Nationale in Paris—these and many others are of priceless value, not only for understanding the history and early stages of the Greek text but also the text of the underlying Hebrew as it existed long before the standardized edition by the Masoretes appeared.

The contents of the Greek Bible, in the three most important copies we possess, are as follows. In Codex Vaticanus the order is:

Genesis	Micah
Exodus	Joel
Leviticus	Obadiah
Numbers	Jonah
Deuteronomy	Nahum
Joshua	Habakkuk
Judges	Zephaniah
Ruth	Haggai
Kingdoms I-IV[1]	Zechariah
Chronicles I-II	Malachi
Esdras I-II[2]	Isaiah
Psalms	Jeremiah
Proverbs	Baruch
Ecclesiastes	Lamentations
Song of Solomon	Epistle of Jeremiah
Job	Ezekiel
Wisdom of Solomon	Daniel
Wisdom of Sirach	
Esther[3]	Matthew
Judith	Mark
Tobit	Luke
Hosea	John
Amos	Acts of the Apostles

[1] i.e., 1-2 Samuel, 1-2 Kings.

[2] Esdr. I is the apocryphal book of 1 Esdras; in the Latin Bible it is known as Esdras III. It stands at the beginning of the English Apocrypha. Esdr. II is a combination of Ezra and Nehemiah; in the Latin Bible these are separated, as in the English, and are known as Esdras I-II.

[3] Including the additions found in the Greek but not in the Hebrew.

James	Corinthians II
Peter I	Galatians
Peter II	Ephesians
John I	Philippians
John II	Colossians
John III	Thessalonians I
Jude	Thessalonians II
Romans	Hebrews[4]
Corinthians I	

Codex Sinaiticus contains the same books as Vaticanus, some of them in a different order, and also has Maccabees I and II, following Judith; at the end of the New Testament it has the Epistle of Barnabas and the Shepherd of Hermas.

Codex Alexandrinus also has the contents of Old and New Testament, in a slightly different order, and includes Maccabees I to IV, instead of the first two books only; and it includes the Odes (i.e., the Canticles found in the Bible, and the *Gloria in Excelsis*) at the end of the Psalter and the Psalms of Solomon at the end of the Old Testament. At the end of the New Testament it has 1 and 2 Clement.

As we have seen, the Septuagint, i.e., the "Greek Version of the Old Testament," is referred to constantly in the footnotes to the Revised Standard Version. The RSV also refers to the Samaritan "Hebrew text of the Old Testament" —i.e., the copies of the Pentateuch which were derived from the text, written in Samaritan or Old Hebrew characters, current about 400 B.C. when the schism between Jews and

[4] Codex Vaticanus breaks off in the middle of Heb. 9:14. It undoubtedly continued with the rest of the New Testament books, as in the other Greek codices, and like them may have included other books as well. The missing books are: Timothy I, Timothy II, Titus, Philemon, Apocalypse of John.

Samaritans took place. There is also a Samaritan Targum, much like the Old Palestinian Targum among the Jews, viz., a translation into currently spoken Aramaic. The RSV also refers to the Syriac, a version of even greater importance for the Old Testament than for the New. Its classic or "authorized" version is known as the *Peshitta*, or "simple" version; it was perhaps based upon, or largely influenced by, the Greek translations, though there is a growing body of evidence to support the view that it was made from the Hebrew. Professor Kahle's theory that the Syriac version originated as the Bible of Syriac (Eastern Aramaic) speaking Jews in Adiabene is a fascinating and probable reconstruction of the origin of this version.[5] Other early versions of the Old Testament are the Coptic, the Ethiopic, and the Latin; but none ranks in importance with the Greek. An illustration will make clear the way in which the Greek and Syriac combine to correct the traditional Hebrew. In Habakkuk 2:16, the Hebrew reads: "Drink, yourself, and be uncircumcised." But the Greek and Syriac have what is obviously and self-evidently no correction but the original: "Drink, yourself, and stagger" (so RSV). There are many other passages where the ancient versions have aided us in restoring the original text. The reader will find a search for them, in the footnotes to the RSV, a most interesting and rewarding study.

Once more, the ancient and continuous *use* of the Bible in the lectionary, in the church's teaching, and in preaching, is obvious. The great codices, including Vaticanus and Sinaiticus, are thought by many scholars to have been among

---

[5] See his book, *The Cairo Geniza*, 2d edition 1959, pp. 265ff.

the fifty copies ordered by the emperor Constantine for the churches of "New Rome," his city on the Bosporus, Constantinople, when the persecutions had ended and Christianity became a recognized religion throughout the Empire. These were de luxe copies, made on vellum, and were meant to last indefinitely. Obviously they were intended for constant use, and were to lie open and be read in the churches. We underestimate the importance attached to the Bible in the ancient church, and also in the Middle Ages, if we forget these facts. In one of St. Augustine's letters he describes the lay folk of his diocese, Hippo in North Africa, gathering daily in the churches to hear the Bible read to them. Close familiarity with the Bible stories is also reflected in the church's art—all the way from the earliest days in the Roman catacombs to the frescoes at Monreale, where the whole Bible is drawn upon for illustrations, or to the mosaic floor of the cathedral at Siena, with its portrayal of the biblical wars. Everywhere, acquaintance with the Bible was taken for granted; and it may very well be true that a fifth- or tenth- or fifteenth-century Christian knew the Bible far better than many a churchgoer in the twentieth, for whom the Bible is a little known, little read book.

The addition of the books of the Greek New Testament to those of the Greek Old Testament was both natural and inevitable, since the practice of reading the Old Testament as a lectionary at public worship was taken over by the Christians from the Jewish synagogue. In fact, the author of the earliest gospel assumes that his book will be read aloud, presumably at worship (see Mark 13:14), and Paul directs that two of his letters shall be read publicly (Col. 4:16; the Epistle to the Laodiceans has not survived). This use of the Christian writings along with the books of the Greek Old Testament must have had a powerful influence upon the formation of the New Testament canon, the Christian supplement to the Jewish Bible, its completion and climax. (This took place long before the time of Marcion, who is often supposed to have been the first to suggest a Christian New Testament to "offset" the Jewish scriptures.) It was henceforth as a whole work that *the* Bible ("the books") now existed, and was translated into various languages, Latin, Syriac, Coptic, Armenian, Gothic, Georgian, and many others, ancient and modern. The very manuscripts show this: not only the great codices, like Vaticanus, Sinaiticus, and Alexandrinus, but the smaller collections or groups of books, often in four volumes, viz., (*a*) the gospels, (*b*) Acts and the Catholic Epistles, (*c*) the Pauline Epistles and Hebrews, (*d*) the Apocalypse.[6] The Bible was always understood (except by Marcionites) to include the Old Testament, and was never complete unless the Old Testament was part of it, with its various groups of books: the Pentateuch, the Earlier and Latter Prophets, the Psalms, the Wisdom books, and the Hagiographa. These groups often had their own distinctive textual history, for they were copied, expounded, translated, revised, and made the subject of commentaries independently of the rest of Scripture. Nevertheless, over all stood the total concept of "the

[6] Among the minuscules (the later Greek manuscripts) the vast majority are gospels: only 46 contain the whole New Testament; ca. 507 contain the Acts and Catholic Epistles; 595 the Pauline letters and Hebrews; 223 the Apocalypse. See H. J. Vogels, *Handbuch der Textkritik des Neuen Testaments*, 2d ed., Bonn, 1955, p. 62. These partial copies were doubtless for convenience in use—as are similar books today. The *lectionary* Bibles were complete.

holy writings," separate and distinct from all other books; and a part was never substituted for the whole. In the ancient church the New Testament was never viewed as "the Bible of the Christians" (as some view it today), for the Bible of the Christians was the Greek Old Testament plus the Greek New Testament, and either was thought to be incomplete without the other. The key to the meaning of each lay in the central message of the other: Christ's predicted coming, and the preparation of the world and of the Jewish people for his coming, on one hand; on the other, his arrival, his life, teaching, death, resurrection, and future coming in glory as the fulfillment of the ancient Law and the prophets.

III.

THE

LATIN

BIBLE

WE COME now to the Latin translation. The principle of interpretation which assumes that the Bible was the church's book, primarily its book read at public worship, is equally sound when we consider the early history of this version. The first occasion for such translation was probably the "lessons" read in church, specifically the Epistles and Gospels at the Eucharist. The translation was done sporadically, here and there, as need arose—much as in churches where the service is in Latin or German or some language not wholly understood by the congregation, and the preacher often translates the Epistle and Gospel (at least the latter) before the sermon at Mass. The evidence for this assertion is the variety in style and vocabulary of the Old Latin version. Many copies, and fragments of copies, of this early version have survived. It presumably began to appear about A.D. 150, when the church had grown strong enough to reach districts outside the

Greek-speaking metropolises. The agreement of the manuscripts with the type of text used by Latin church fathers enables us to locate them. Thus the Old Latin version of Mark and Matthew in the Codex Bobbiensis ($=k$) found at Bobbio and now at Turin, and assigned by experts to the fourth or fifth century, is almost identical with the type of text used by St. Cyprian of Carthage, martyred A.D. 258. Strange to say, the Old Latin translation agrees closely with the Old Syriac, as represented in the two manuscripts found, one in the British Museum and edited by William Cureton (in 1858), and the other on Mt. Sinai (in 1892) by Agnes Smith Lewis and her sister Margaret Dunlop Gibson. This connection between Carthage and the West, on one hand, and Antioch and the East, on the other, is one of the mysteries of textual history. Perhaps the solution was partly economic: these areas were closely affiliated by trade, in the opening centuries of the Christian era. All along, trade and transport had much to do with the spread of Christianity and the dissemination of the Scriptures.

But the time came when the Old Latin New Testament, especially the gospels, required revision. Private copies, i.e., copies made by or for private owners, were looked upon as purely personal property—there was no copyright in the ancient world. And so it often happened that an owner of a gospel, or of more than one, would add to his copy what he had heard read from one of the other gospels, on the theory that all being equally true and accurate, it was desirable to have each as complete as possible. The same view evidently held also in Syria and elsewhere: we frequently find words and phrases, and even the order of verses, taken over from Matthew, which was viewed as the "apostolic" gospel *par excellence* and, therefore, the standard to which the others should be conformed. Readings from John, likewise, were inserted into the other gospels, notably Luke; though in this case, interestingly, the "Western" type of manuscripts did *not* make the insertions (see p. 119).

And so, in the year 384, Pope Damasus commissioned his secretary, Jerome, a thoroughly competent Greek and Latin scholar, to make a revision of the New Testament, beginning with the gospels. We still possess the letter addressed to Pope Damasus which Jerome prefaced to his revision. It reflects his hesitation and reluctance to begin the task, and his realization that the step would bring sharp criticism upon him. It also describes the method he pursued in preparing the revision.

JEROME TO POPE DAMASUS

You have urged me to make a new work out of an old, and to sit in judgment, as it were, on the copies of the scriptures which are now scattered throughout the whole world; and, inasmuch as they differ from one another, you would have me decide which of them agree with the Greek original. This is a labor of piety, but at the same time one of dangerous presumption; for in judging others I will myself be judged by all; and how dare I change the language of the world's old age and carry it back to the days of its childhood? Who is there, whether learned or unlearned, who, when he takes up the volume in his hands and discovers that what he reads therein does not agree with what he is accustomed to, will not break out at once in a loud voice and call me a sacrilegious forger, for daring to add something to the ancient books, to make changes and corrections in them?

On the other hand, there are two considerations which console me: in the first place, the order comes from you, who are the supreme pontiff [*summus sacerdos*]; secondly, even those who speak against us have to admit that divergent readings cannot [all] be right. For if we are to pin our faith to the Latin copies, our opponents must tell us *which;* for there are almost as many forms of text as there are copies [*tot sunt paene quot codices*]. If, on the other hand, we are to search out the truth by a comparison of many, why not go back to the original Greek and correct the mistakes introduced either by inaccurate translators or by the blundering emendations of self-confident but ignorant critics, or the additions and changes made by copyists who were only half-awake?

I am not discussing the Old Testament, which was turned into Greek by the Seventy Elders, and has come down to us by three stages. I do not ask what Aquila and Symmachus think, or why Theodotion takes a middle course between the ancients and the moderns: let that be the true translation which the apostles approved! But I am speaking now of the New Testament, which was undoubtedly composed in Greek, with the exception of [the work of] the Apostle Matthew, who first in Judea set forth the Gospel of Christ in Hebrew letters. Since in our language [the New Testament] is certainly discordant, the stream flowing in different channels, we must go back to the source. I pass over those manuscripts which bear the names of Lucian and Hesychius, whose authority is perversely maintained by some. Certainly these writers could not amend anything in the Old Testament that the Seventy had approved; nor could they succeed in amending the new, as versions of scripture already existing in the languages of many nations would show that their additions were false. Therefore in this short Preface I promise only the four Gospels, whose order is Matthew, Mark, Luke, John, revised by comparison with the Greek manuscripts—i.e., the old ones. But lest they should differ too greatly from the Latin which we are accustomed to read, I have restrained my pen, correcting [only] such passages as seemed to change the meaning but allowing the rest to remain as they were.

[The Preface continues with a description of the ten "canons" or tables drawn up by Eusebius of Caesarea, following Ammonius of Alexandria, for the purpose of comparing the passages in the four gospels which were in close agreement—a kind of early "Harmony of the Gospels." [1] He then concludes:]

I trust that in Christ you are well, and that you will remember me, *Papa beatissime!*

The anticipated opposition arose, and followed him all his life. But the Pope's encouragement had been enough to launch the project—though Damasus had died that very year—and Jerome went on to revise or translate the rest of the Bible. His basis was still the Greek text, though eventually he learned Hebrew in order to translate the Old Testament. The translation found in the Old Latin *Old* Testament was far less reliable than that in the New. But again, the agreements with the Old Syriac are frequent, and important. Since Jerome did not accept the Apocrypha as part of Scripture—nor did the Syrian church—he declined to revise them, and so to this day the Latin Bible contains the Old Latin version of these books. In fact it was a century or more before Jerome's version finally ousted the Old Latin

---

[1] The original text of this letter can be found in Wordsworth and White's *Latin New Testament* (Oxford University Press, 1911 and later).

from common use in the West, and some even of the New Testament books continued to be copied and used in the Old Latin version for several centuries. Codex Colbertinus (*c*) of the gospels, in Paris, dates from the twelfth century; Corbeiensis (*ff*[1]), in Petrograd, from the eleventh; Sangermanensis (*g*[2]), in Paris, from the tenth. One manuscript of the Acts and Catholic Epistles dates from the thirteenth century, and another from the fifteenth! Jerome made three revisions of the Psalter, later known as the Roman, the Gallican, and the Hebrew. The first was his early revision of the Old Latin on the basis of the Septuagint; the second was based on the Hexaplar Greek text of Origen, as was also his revision of the Book of Job, where the Hebrew is specially difficult; the third was based on the Hebrew original, after he had mastered that language.

The fullest explanation of his method is set forth in the "Helmeted Preface" to his translation of Samuel and Kings, the first of his prefaces to be published (A.D. 391). It was addressed to Paula and her daughter Eustochium, two Roman ladies, friends of Jerome, who had adopted the ascetic life and had come to Palestine in order to be near their teacher; they were zealous students of Holy Scripture.[2]

THE "HELMETED PREFACE"
TO SAMUEL AND KINGS

That the Hebrews have twenty-two letters is attested by the Syriac and Chaldean [i.e., Aramaic] languages, which are closely related to it; for they have twenty-two elementary sounds, pronounced in the same way [as the Hebrew] but written with different characters. The Samaritans also use

---

[2] The passage may be found in Migne's *Patrologia Latina*, Vol. 28 = Hieronymus, Vol. IX, 547-558.

the same number of letters in their [copies of the] Pentateuch of Moses; these differ only in their shape and form
[*figuris tantum et apicibus*]. It is also certain that Esdras
[Ezra], the scribe and teacher of the Law, after the capture
of Jerusalem and the restoration of the temple under Zerub-
babel, invented other letters [the "square" Hebrew alphabet]
which we now use, although up to that time the Samaritan
and the Hebrew characters were identical. In the Book of
Numbers [3:39] also, where we have the census of the priests
and Levites, the mystic teaching of scripture leads us to
the same conclusion [there were 22,000 in all]. And in some
Greek books we find the four-lettered [*tetragrammaton*]
name of the Lord [YHWH] written to this day in the
ancient characters. The 37th Psalm, moreover, the 111th,
the 112th, the 119th, and the 145th, although they are
written in different metres, have as their acrostic pattern
an alphabet with the same number of letters. The Lamentations of Jeremiah and his Prayer, the Proverbs of Solomon
also, towards the end—the passage beginning "Who will
find a brave woman?" [31:10]—are instances of the same
[number of letters in the] alphabet, forming the division into
sections [or verses]. Again, five letters are double, viz.,
Caph, Mem, Nun, Phe, Sade; for at the beginning and in
the middle of words they are written one way and at the end
another. From this it comes to pass that by most persons
five of the books are reckoned as double, viz., Samuel, Kings,
Chronicles, Ezra [i.e., including Nehemiah], Jeremiah (i.e.,
including *Kinōth,* his Lamentations). As then there are
twenty-two elementary characters by means of which we
write whatever we say, and the compass of the human voice
is contained within their limits, so we reckon twenty-two
books, by which, as by an alphabet of letters and the beginning of learning the righteous are instructed in the doctrine

of God from tender infancy and as if still nursed at the breast.

[Jerome continues by describing the contents of the Old Testament, the five books of Torah or Law, i.e., the Pentateuch; the Prophets, i.e., Joshua, Judges, Samuel, Kings, which the Jews call the Former Prophets, and Isaiah, Jeremiah, Ezekiel, the Twelve ("Minor" or shorter prophets), which the Jews call the Latter Prophets; the Hagiographa, which the Jews call the "Writings," and which include the rest of the canonical Old Testament. These twenty-four (not twenty-two!) books Jerome says were symbolized by the "four and twenty elders" in the Apocalypse of John, who adore the Lamb and offer him their crowns (Rev. 4:4, 10). He then continues:]

This preface to the scriptures may serve as a "helmeted" introduction [*prologus . . . quasi galeatus*] to all the books which we turn from Hebrew into Latin; we want you to assume that what is not found in our list must be placed among the "apocryphal" writings. The Book of Wisdom, therefore, which is commonly ascribed to Solomon, and the Book of Jesus the Son of Sirach, and Judith, and Tobias [Tobit], and the Shepherd [of Hermas] are not in the canon. The First Book of Maccabees I have found to be Hebrew; the second is Greek, as can be proved from its very style. Seeing that all this is so, I beg you, my reader, not to suppose that my labors are in any sense intended to disparage the ancient translators. For in the service of the tabernacle of God each one offers what he can: some gold and silver and precious stones, others linen and blue and scarlet [see Exodus 25—26]; we shall do well if we offer skins and goats' hair [Exod. 26:14]. And yet the Apostle pronounces our more contemptible parts the more necessary [I Cor. 12:22]. Accordingly, the beauty of the whole tabernacle and of its various parts—distinguishing the present and the future church—was covered with skins and goats' hair cloths [*pellibus . . . et ciliciis*], and so the heat of the sun and the injurious rain were warded off by those things which were of less account. [Jerome hopes his work will be useful if not beautiful!]

First, then, read my Samuel and Kings: mine, I say, *mine!* For whatever by diligent translation and by careful emendation we have learned and made our own is ours. And when you understand that about which you were formerly ignorant, you may, if you are grateful, esteem me a translator, or, if ungrateful, a paraphraser; however, I am not in the least conscious of having deviated from the Hebrew original [*de Hebraica veritate*]. At all events, if you are incredulous, read the Greek and Latin manuscripts and compare them with these modest efforts of mine; and wherever you find that they disagree, ask any Hebrew, in whom you must have more confidence [than in me], and if he confirms our view, I suppose you will not think him a soothsayer and assume that he and I have, in rendering the same passage, divined alike. But I also ask you, Paula and Eustochium, handmaidens of Christ who anoint the head of your reclining Lord with the most precious ointment of faith [see John 12:3], who by no means seek the Saviour in the tomb [see Luke 24:5], for whom Christ has already ascended to the Father [see John 20:17]—I beg you to confront with the shields of your prayers the mad dogs who bark and rage against me and go about the city [Psalm 59:6, 14] and in this think themselves learned if they disparage others. I, knowing my lowliness, will always remember the saying:

I said, I will take heed to my ways,
   that I sin not with my tongue.

I have set a guard upon my mouth,
  so long as the sinner is standing against me.
I became dumb, and was humbled, and kept silence,
  [even] from good [words]. (Psalm 39:1-3)

[Jerome's version of the Psalm differs from most others.]

Jerome began by explaining why there are just 22 books of the Old Testament (later he shifted the number to 24). The explanation reminds us of St. Irenaeus's argument that there can be only four gospels, as there are only four cardinal directions, four winds, four beasts in the Apocalypse, and so on. This kind of "mystical" or "allegorical," not to say "typological" or even "numerological" exposition was very popular in the ancient church—and in wide areas of the contemporary ancient Greek and Latin literary scene.

It is very evident that St. Jerome endured the "trials of a translator"—to borrow the title of Fr. Ronald Knox's fascinating book. But he bore up manfully, and his version in the common speech, *Biblia vulgata*, became the Bible of the Western world for a thousand years, and is to this day the standard version in the Roman Catholic Church. It is often described as "the queen of the versions," and it fully deserves that title. It was made by a scholar who *spoke* both Greek and Latin, and whose Hebrew was learned from experts, Palestinian rabbis and teachers who also were interested in precision and accuracy of rendering.

The influence of Jerome's renderings, in both Old Testament and New, upon Western theology down to the Reformation, and long past the Reformation in the Roman Church, is obvious and undeniable. For example, his rendering of John's message in Matt. 3:2 is *Paenitentiam agite:* "Do *penance,*" instead of the simple Greek *metanoeite,* "Repent." In the Lord's Prayer (Matt. 6:9-13) he introduced *panem nostrum supersubstantialem,* "our supersubstantial bread," though two later (ninth-century) manuscripts still read the Old Latin *cotidianum,* "daily," and some even conflated the two: "supersubstantial daily bread." Jerome himself later explained, after he had learned Hebrew, that the Greek *epiousion* merely represented the Semitic term *mahar,* "of the morrow." The "daily bread" for which we all pray was eaten, as a rule, and certainly among the peasantry of Palestine, on the "morrow"; for the day began at sundown, and the ancient peasants' one main meal of the day followed. Thus today's bread, "eaten by the sweat of his face" and as the result of hard toil (Gen. 3:19), was eaten, one might say, "tomorrow," and was so prayed for. But in the Vulgate Jerome had read into the phrase a reference to the Eucharist, as many devout souls still do, to this day. The phrase in vs. 12, "Forgive us our debts, as we forgive our debtors," is still the basic rendering commonly used in English—rather than "as we have forgiven" (which is required by vv. 14f, and is the RSV rendering of the Greek *aphēkamen*).

Even more crucial was Jerome's interpretation—or retention—of the last petition (v. 13), "And lead us not into temptation, but deliver us from evil": *et ne nos inducas* (where the Old Latin had *passus fueris induci nos*) *in tentationem, sed libera nos a malo.* The Old Latin, "Suffer us not to be led into trial," is both biblical and liturgical in style (see Tertullian, *On Prayer,* 8). Compare the end of "Notker's hymn," the medieval Swiss dirge still included in the Burial Office: "Suffer us not, at our last hour, for any

44 ·

pains of death, to fall from thee"; or the prayer "For our Country" in the prayers at the end of Evening Prayer: "In the day of trouble, suffer not our trust in thee to fail." (The Prayer Book as a whole is a most excellent commentary on the Lord's Prayer!) But the language has been transformed by centuries of use, and the influence of St. Augustine, for whom faith was a divine gift, not a human undertaking, is very evident. (The idea that faith is a supernatural gift is not clearly stated in the New Testament. Luke 17:5, "Increase our faith!" is a petition of the disciples, while "Help my unbelief!" in Mark 9:24 is the puzzled, paradoxical appeal of a distracted father.)

In modern Western languages, where "temptation" means a diabolical inducement to commit a sin, the phrase leads to great difficulty. This was evident not long ago when a proposal was made to the General Convention of the Episcopal Church that the Prayer Book version of the Lord's Prayer should be changed to read, "Do not permit us to yield to temptation," or something similar. But the Greek *peirasmos* does not mean "temptation," in the modern sense; it means testing or trial (see Sirach 2:1, explained in the five following verses, 2-6). Neither did *tentatio* in the Latin of Jerome's day; it meant "attempt," "trial," or even "proof." And the Greek word *eisenegkēs* (from *eispherō*, not from *eisagō*) did not mean "lead into" but "cause or permit to enter," *sino intrare;* and in the context, in a petition addressed to God, it surely means "Do not put us to the test: do not subject us to the kind or degree of tribulation that tries men's souls and breaks down their faith." The line in the old hymn catches this nuance of meaning exactly: "When through the deep waters I call thee to go" ("cause,"

· 45

which is sometimes sung, would be better than "call"). The whole idea is the trial or testing of the valiant—as Abraham, like many another, according to Jewish teaching, was put to the test;[3] and it is a petition *not* to be tried or tested above what we are able to bear (1 Cor. 10:13) ; and the "evil" from which we pray to be delivered, is not the "evil one" (Satan) or the "evil neighbor" of a well-known Jewish prayer, but the evils (plural) of life which break men down and destroy their confidence in God. Once more, let us turn to the Book of Common Prayer. In the first collect in the Litany we say: "Graciously hear us, that *those evils* which the craft and subtlety of the devil or man worketh against us, may, by thy good providence, be brought to naught; that we thy servants, being hurt by no *persecutions*, may evermore give thanks unto thee in thy holy Church." The idea that Satan causes evils, including persecution and martyrdom, as a trial or test of men's faith (see Job 1—2, for sickness, calamity, and disaster as trials by Satan) is assumed throughout the New Testament and elsewhere in early Christian literature—for example in the stories of the martyrs.

This is the "evil" we read of, repeatedly, in the Old Testament, especially the Psalms. It was the total contradiction of the basic assumption of much Old Testament teach-

[3] The trials of Abraham were listed and studied in the Jewish schools in the same way as Greek teachers made the labors of Heracles the basis of moral instruction. They were a prototype of the "trials" of the nation (on which see, e.g., Ps. 66:10-12 = BCP vv. 9-11). The Lord's Prayer is, of course, a community or "common" prayer, not solely individual: it begins "*Our* Father" and is like the Shortened Shemoneh Esreh in Judaism, said every day. The "evil" and the "trials" are national or social, not merely private and personal; see Lam. 1:13 (national) and Isa. 43:2—the "fire and water" of Keans's hymn.

ing. As Lord Francis Bacon said, in his *Essays* (edition of 1612; Essay V), "Prosperity is the blessing of the Old Testament, adversity is the blessing of the New." When the Christian disciple is taught to pray for deliverance from evil, it is with the scene in Gethsemane before his mind's eye, and with the words of his Lord echoing in his inmost being: "*Abba*, Father, all things are possible to thee; remove this cup from me; yet not what I will, but what thou wilt" (Mark 14:36). Jesus himself gives the explanation of the petition in the words that follow (v. 38), "Watch [*or* keep awake] and pray that you may not enter into temptation; the spirit indeed is willing, but the flesh is weak"—as the church discovered, in Mark's time and later, when the prospect of martyrdom confronted many a weak and terrified Christian, some of them only recent converts. Mark's *parenegke* ("remove," "take away") in v. 36, which is a verb formed on the same root as *eisenegkēs*, and therefore related to it, is translated by Jerome as *transfer;* and in v. 38 he has *ut non intretis in tentationem.* The precise nuance of the Greek is difficult to state in Latin—or in English. Perhaps "Do not subject us to trial" (i.e., beyond our strength) or, "Do not put us to the test," would convey it better; but this is scarcely a possible revision of the current version of the Lord's Prayer. Only, let us say, the clergy and the Church's other teachers might perhaps do well to give us more frequent expositions of such common and universally used phrases as those of the Lord's Prayer.

Down through the centuries, then, Jerome's "common version," the Vulgate, steadily won its way. Its literary as well as its theological influence was paramount. It became *the* Bible of the West. The Roman Mass, the Breviary, the

Latin hymns, Dante, St. Thomas, and all the Schoolmen, the earliest translators into English and other Western languages—all used the Vulgate, up to the rise of the modern national literatures of Western Europe. And even later, as we have seen, its influence continued, and the understanding of the Greek New Testament and even of the Hebrew Old Testament has been affected by it. Not only the sermons of the Reformers and of those who followed them—Bishop Lancelot Andrewes, for example, in the seventeenth century, or John Donne of St. Paul's, preachers who slipped from English to Latin and Latin to English with the greatest of ease—but also the devotions of Anglicans as well as Roman Catholics, and even of Lutherans and Calvinists, were often phrased in the Latin of St. Jerome's Bible—and of St. Augustine's *Sermons, Confessions*, and prayers.

IV.

THE

ENGLISH

BIBLE

1. To Wycliffe

It is commonly believed, in some places, that the Bible was totally unknown during the Dark and Middle Ages, that it was in fact "withheld from the people" before the Reformation, and that only a few apocryphal or greatly garbled Bible stories trickled through to the laity from the friars' preaching. But, as we have seen, this delusion leaves unexplained the popular art, drama, poetry, and music of those centuries, and also the transmission of the manuscripts. As a matter of fact, the Bible was fairly well known all through the long centuries stretching from the barbarian invasions and the fall of Rome to the beginnings of the Renaissance and the Reformation. Even Greek was known and read in some places, e.g., in Ireland—and some would say Hebrew too. There were Greek and Hebrew manuscripts in Alcuin's library at York—the best library in Western Europe, destroyed by William the Conqueror when he "harried the North" in 1069. Long before then there were translations into various Western languages, though the Latin Vulgate was the official Bible used in church services and in schools. And it was the Vulgate, in the currently accepted form of text, which was the basis of translation. About A.D. 700, a century after St. Augustine of Canterbury, the missionary to "Angle-land," had arrived in Britain, the beautiful Lindisfarne Gospels were copied; and two centuries or more later an interlinear translation in Anglo-Saxon was added to them, somewhere near Durham. The poet Caedmon (circa A.D. 670) sang his simple songs in alliterative verse, recounting the Bible stories as he had heard them from the monks at Whitby in Yorkshire. Such poetical paraphrases were common for centuries, but only a few fragments have survived. In A.D. 735 the saintly scholar Bede, "the Venerable," translated the Gospel of John on his deathbed. The dramatic story of his final effort, only finishing the translation as he drew his last breath, has often been told. The first account was by St. Cuthbert, who was present when the scholar died.

It was the Eve of Ascension Day. Bede lay ill and dying in his monastic cell at Jarrow, but dictating, as his strength slowly ebbed away, the final chapters of the Gospel. While his disciples were writing he urged them to hurry, for his end had come, and he knew not how much or how little time was left. On the morning of Ascension Day only one chapter remained to be done [presumably the short chapter in the Vulgate, not our longer Chapter 21]. The young monk who had been writing hesitated to urge Bede to continue, but the scholar insisted. "Take your pen and write quickly—it can be finished." But the brethren came in to bid their master farewell, and the day was thus spent before they realized it. At last the young copyist reminded him, "There is only one sentence more," and Bede replied, "Write quickly." "Now it is written," said the boy; and the master answered, "Yes, you speak truly; it is finished—now." He bade them take him from his bed and lay him on the floor of the cell, supporting his head with their hands. Repeating the *Gloria Patri* he died, his last word being the name of God the Holy Spirit.

Unfortunately, not a single trace of Bede's translation has been preserved. A century later (circa 825), the "Vespasian Psalter" was produced by inserting an Anglo-Saxon version between the lines of the Latin text of the Psalms. There are similar manuscript books from the ninth to the twelfth centuries. They were not really translations so much as interlinear glosses, of the kind often added to textbooks by schoolboys studying Latin or Greek. A genuine attempt at a translation of the Psalms was made by King Alfred (circa 890) but he died when he had finished only the first part. In his *Book of Laws* he incorporated a translation of passages from Exodus 20—23, beginning with the Ten Commandments, and also some from the Book of Acts.

The liturgical significance of most early English translations is clear from the books chosen: chiefly the Psalms and the Gospels. That these books are usually the first to be translated, and the longest to survive, is clear evidence of their importance in public worship. One of the most striking incidents in Marco Polo's account of his journey to China and long residence there, in the thirteenth century, is his discovery of a dwindling colony of Chinese Christians belonging to the Eastern (i.e., Nestorian) Church. Their other books had all been destroyed, but their religion still survived, nourished upon a copy of the Old Testament Psalter!

Thus the tenth century saw not only the Northumbrian gloss added to the Lindisfarne Gospels, and the Mercian gloss to the Rushworth Gospels (also in Yorkshire), but also the Four Gospels translated into West Saxon by first-rate Latin and Saxon scholars. These gospels were among the first Anglo-Saxon books to be printed, John Foxe producing an edition in 1571. Late in the tenth century the Abbot Aelfric translated considerable parts of the Old Testament into Anglo-Saxon, viz., the Pentateuch, Joshua, Judges, Kings, Esther, Job, Judith, and Maccabees; in brief, the historical books, for the most part, and in form a "Shorter Bible," as he omitted the less important or less interesting passages. Such courageous editorial excisions could be made only by a scholar who was also Archbishop of Canterbury; even so he regretted ever having put his hand to the task!—that is, if Abbot and Archbishop were one and the same man; this is disputed. His monastery lay just west of Oxford, at Eynsham. Nothing remains of it today except a few stones which have been built into a modern house. Of his translations from the Bible, only two manuscripts contain the Hexateuch; the rest are fragmentary. So man perishes, and all his works—even his good works; but the word of the Lord abides for ever.

The Anglo-Saxon Bible thus contained the Hexateuch and several other Old Testament books, the Psalms (fifty in prose, the rest in metre), and the Gospels; of the rest, the

Book of Acts, the Epistles, and the Apocalypse were found only in fragmentary translations as cited in homilies. There is also a surviving fragment of a version of the apocryphal Gospel of Nicodemus. But the translations were made only, it appears, at the request of the laity: the monks and clergy knew Latin and could read the Vulgate. It is interesting to note that Ramsey Abbey in Huntingdonshire possessed the whole Old Testament in Hebrew. No doubt the copy once belonged to an English Jew or to a Jewish synagogue.

Towards the close of the twelfth century a literary revival took place, in what is known as Middle English. Characteristically, the first biblical book to appear in the new language was the Psalter, again in a northern dialect, and in metre (circa 1300). A little later came versions in prose, one of them by the mystic, Richard Rolle of Hampole, who added a commentary to his translation. Richard Rolle died in 1349, but his work continued in use for a century or more. Once again, the sporadic translation or paraphrase of the Sunday Gospels led the way, and prepared for full translations of the Gospels into Middle English.

In the early part of the fourteenth century Nicolas of Lyra (d. 1340) emphasized the importance of the literal meaning of Scripture, as contrasted with the traditional fourfold interpretation favored in the West. For centuries, preachers had exercised their imagination, devout or otherwise, upon the text of Scripture, often producing strange and unrecognizable exegesis. Their rule was summarized:

> *Littera gesta docet,*
> *Quid credas, allegoria;*
> *Moralis, quid agat,*
> *Quid speres, anagogia.*

("The literal interpretation tells what took place; the allegorical what you are to believe; the moral what you are to do; the anagogical what you may hope for!") But now a movement had begun in the direction of simplicity and directness. It was destined to grow, until in the sixteenth century the Protestant Reformers insisted upon the "plain and simple" interpretation of Holy Scripture, and the literal, historical, original meaning of its language. Martin Luther himself looked back and gave credit to Nicolas of Lyra:

> *Si Lyra non lyrasset*
> *Lutherus non saltasset.*

("If Nicolas had not struck up his lyre, Luther would never have danced.")

In England the movement got under way in the work of John Wycliffe (1328-84), who demanded a fresh and literal translation of the Vulgate Bible as a guide to the Law of the Kingdom. His teaching at Balliol College, Oxford, his preaching at Lutterworth where he was rector, his organization of groups of young men, students at Oxford, to go about the country and preach repentance and a return to primitive gospel teaching, resulted in a profound change in the temper and outlook of the English people, and prepared for the Reformation which followed a little over a century later. Wycliffe's life was uneventful, thanks to the powerful protection of his patron, John of Gaunt, Duke of Lancaster; nevertheless, strong forces of ecclesiastical and political conservatism were arrayed against him and his "poor preachers." In order to make clear the inspired authority for his principles of reform, he began the translation of the whole Bible into Middle English—it was the English of Chaucer's *Canterbury Tales*. He was assisted by two of his followers, Nicholas of Hereford and John Purvey. This literal translation (1384) was followed by a freer one after Wycliffe's death, the work being carried on by Hereford and Purvey (1385-87).

By the "Law of God" Wycliffe meant the law set forth in the Old and New Testament, as contrasted with papal pronouncements and traditions. The church, he held, is one and indivisible, with Christ as its true and only Head. It is invisible, and its membership is limited to the elect (views which were later identified with Lutheranism and Calvinism); salvation is a consequence of predestination and grace rather than of baptism and membership in the church; a "priesthood of all believers" must take the place of the historic Christian ministry; royal power is derived directly from God, for the purpose of administering justice and protecting the weak; the clergy must therefore obey the law of the land and the commands of the sovereign—for they hold their "temporalities" of office only by royal consent, and even the pope must acknowledge this principle; the pope deserves respect only when he acts as a Christian should; and the Bible is the sole standard and rule of life, for king and country and for the individual Christian.

The very language used by Wycliffe, "the morning star of the Reformation," anticipates several of the issues raised four generations later. The place of the Bible and of its literal, verbal, historical interpretation in this new movement toward reform is also clear. What Eduard Meyer called the "anthropological" background of history (see p. 6), including the social and political, the economic and psy-

chological, is nowhere more fully presupposed than in Wycliffe's work; nor is the revolution in modern historical writing anywhere more evident than in the present-day view of
Wycliffe. His views were destined to prevail and to grow
more extreme, even in his own lifetime, and especially in
the application made of them by his "Lollard" followers.
Wycliffe himself could not understand why so much fuss
was made over his teaching, which he believed to be the
simple doctrine of the Bible, or why "every sparrow twitter-
eth about it."

That the idea of making the Bible available to every layman in England, in his own language, was Wycliffe's own is
evident from all his writings and from the charges brought
against him by his enemies, who opposed not only his particular views on church and state but the entire principle of a
vernacular Bible. The consequences of placing the Bible in
the hands of the laity were too dangerous, uncertain, and
far-reaching! That Wycliffe himself completed only a rela-
tively small part of the translation is clear from a comparison of the Wycliffite Bible (or what remains of it) with
biblical passages quoted in Wycliffe's tracts and sermons and
his translation of the Sunday Gospels. They do not agree!
The same phenomenon was evident in St. Jerome's commentaries on the Bible, where he often quoted another version
than the Vulgate—and also in his three translations of the
Psalter, later known as the Roman, the Gallican, and the
Hebrew. But in Wycliffe's case there are two versions of
that portion of the Old Testament which begins with Genesis
and continues to the middle of Baruch 3:20. One manuscript
of this translation, now in the Bodleian Library at Oxford
(Bodley 959), was certainly dictated to five different scribes,

some of whom were still dominated by what they had been accustomed to write. "That the manuscript is the original is proved by the fact that in numerous instances the renderings have been changed during the progress of the sentence; sometimes an erasure has been made as soon as a word was written, or even before it was completed, and another expression has been substituted. An immediate copy of this (MS. Douce 369) ends with the same words, and adds *Explicit translacionem Nicholay de herford.*" [1] There can be no doubt that Nicholas of Hereford and John Purvey were the continuators of Wycliffe's work, and were the men mainly responsible for the "Wycliffite" versions current in the following century. The place of these versions in the history of the English Bible is important, especially for their service in making the contents of the Bible known to generations who could no longer read the old Anglo-Saxon versions, and in influencing the minds of men during the critical century which led up to and prepared for the Protestant Reformation.

The spirit of Wycliffe's version is always vigorous and direct. The Parable of the Wedding Guests in Matthew 22 provides a good example of the style. The text is from Bagster's *English Hexapla* (London 1841).

MATTHEW 22:1—14 IN WYCLIFFE'S VERSION

AND ihesus answerde and spak eftsones in parablis to hem and seide. The kyngdom of heuenes is made like to a kyng that made weddingis to his sone/ and he sente hise seruantis for to clepe men that weren beden to the weddyngis: and

---

[1] See Sir William Craigie, in H. W. Robinson, *The Bible in its Ancient and English Versions* (Oxford, 1940), p. 139.

they wolden not come/ eftsones he sente other seruantis: and seide/ seye ye to the men that ben beden to the feest/ lo I haue made redi my mete my bolis and my volatilis ben slayn, and alle thingis ben redi: come ye to the weddyngis/ but thei dispiseden/ and wenten forth, oon to his toun/ another to his marchaundise/ but other helden hise seruantis, and turmentiden hem and slowen/ but the king whanne he hadde herde: was wroth/ and he sente his oostis and he distroiede the manquellers and brente her citees/ thanne he seide to hise seruantis/ the weddyngis ben redi: but thei that weren clepid to the feest wer not worthi/ therfore go ye in to the endis of weies: and whom ever ye fynden, clepe ye to the weddyngis/ and hise seruantis yeden out in to weies: and gaderiden to gidre alle that thei founden good and yuel/ and the bridal was fulfillid with men sitting at the mete/ and the kyng entrid to se men sittynge at the mete: and he siye there a man not clothid with bride clooth/ and he seide to hym/ Frend hou entridist thou hidir, with out bride clothis/ and he was doumbe/ thanne the kyng bade his mynystris/ bynde hym bothe hondis and feet: and sende ye him in to vttirmore derknessis/ there schal be wepynge and grentynge of teeth/ for many ben clepid but fewe ben chosen.

Only Tyndale (in 1534) could improve on this vigor and directness; for example, when the king came in "he spyed there a man"—James Moffatt pronounced the phrase perfect.

2. The Sixteenth Century

There were probably hundreds of copies of the Wycliffite Bible in circulation in the fifteenth century. In spite of royal and papal opposition, copies were to be found in royal, ducal, and private possession—and perhaps also papal! There was a veritable "hunger for the word," and it is recorded that as much as £40 was paid for a copy—easily worth ten times that amount in today's currency, not discounting modern inflation; for it took many months for a copyist to prepare a whole Bible manuscript. "Some gave a load of hay," it is said, "for a few chapters of St. James or of St. Paul in English." Parliament tried to prohibit the circulation of the new version, but John of Gaunt blocked the motion. In 1408 the Provincial Council at Oxford, inspired and led by Archbishop Arundel, did succeed in the prohibition of any translation made by a private person "on his own authority"—as if any public or official translation was thereby endangered!—"under pain of the greater excommunication." Yet most of the surviving copies of Purvey's revision of the Wycliffite version were made after 1409! "So mightily grew the word of God and prevailed" (Acts 19:20).

It was the invention of printing that speeded the process, and eventually rendered ineffective such prohibitions as Archbishop Arundel's—though the victory was costly. In 1414 the Council of Constance forbade all vernacular translations; but in 1430 a Spanish translation, the "Bible of the House of Alba," was completed. In 1454, the year after the fall of Constantinople, Gutenberg began using movable type in printing; in 1456 he produced his famous and beautiful Mazarin Bible, so named because a copy was later identified in Cardinal Mazarin's library. Thus the first printed book in Europe was the Latin Bible. There are copies in the Library of Congress at Washington, in the Library of the General Theological Seminary in New York, in the Morgan Library, in the British Museum, and elsewhere. Only about 50 copies still survive, and of these about half are fragmentary.

It is strange that the Wycliffite Bible was not printed—not until 1850. But the reason is not far to seek. As Sir Thomas More observed in 1529:

I thynk ther wyll no prynter lyghtely be so hote to put eny byble in prent at hys own charge, wherof the losse sholde lye hole in hys owne necke, and than hange uppon a doutfull tryall whyther the fyrst copy of hys translacyon was made before Wyclyffys dayes or synnys. For yf yt were made synnys, yt must be approved byfore the pryntynge.[1]

For the same reason the first English translations to be printed from type were printed on the Continent, and copies smuggled into England as merchandise. The cost of printing was defrayed, it appears, by interested laymen, merchants in the City of London. The fierce opposition to William Tyndale's New Testament (1525) is partly explained by his defiance of the Oxford prohibition of 1409, and partly by the harsh tone of criticism introduced into his marginal

[1] See J. Isaacs in H. W. Robinson, *The Bible in its Ancient and English Versions*, p. 149.

notes. The translation, beautiful as it was, and a great improvement over earlier sporadic versions, was nevertheless an instrument of propaganda, not designed to conciliate or to win the approval of the civil and ecclesiastical authorities. But the notes came later.

At first Tyndale had hoped for ecclesiastical permission and approval. After taking his degree at Oxford and studying (probably Greek) for a time at Cambridge, he became tutor to the children of Sir John Walsh, near Bristol, where he found the country clergy quite unlearned; they gathered in the ale-houses and condemned him as a heretic! Taking with him a translation of one of the orations of Isocrates, which he had prepared as evidence of his knowledge of Greek, he went up to London (1523) and called on the bishop, Cuthbert Tunstall. But the bishop put him off, pretending that he already had more dependent clergy in his house than he could support, and telling him to find something else to do in London. Fortunately, he found a patron in Humphrey Monmouth, a rich cloth merchant who had business connections abroad, and with him Tyndale remained for six months, working steadily on "his book" (the New Testament translation). When Tyndale left for Hamburg at the end of this time, Monmouth gave him £10, and some other men—also London merchants, we believe—gave an equal amount. Reaching Germany in 1524, Tyndale proceeded to Wittenberg, where Melanchthon was Professor of Greek and where Luther was occasionally to be seen. Here he probably continued his translation. It was influenced, certainly, by Luther's translation—a work of genius which had been turned out in two and a half months (December 1521—February 1522) while Luther was in protective custody in the Wartburg, under the care of his friend Frederick the Wise. Meanwhile, Henry VIII was urging the dukes of Saxony to forbid the printing of Luther's Bible, and in view of the growing danger Tyndale and his amanuensis, Friar William Roye, moved to Cologne, where a spy discovered that 6,000 copies of Tyndale's "translation of Luther" were being printed and would be sent to England. The printing had gone as far as signature K.

Learning of the new threat to their safety, Tyndale and Roye fled down the Elbe and up the Rhine to Worms, taking with them the sheets already printed. All that survives of this earliest printing is a copy of signatures A-H, in the British Museum. It contains Matt. 1—22, but not the title page. In Worms the printing was continued and copies began arriving in England early in 1526, where Cardinal Wolsey organized a concerted effort to prevent the sale and distribution. But there was no way to stop it. Pirated editions appeared in Holland, and undercover agents arranged the distribution and sale. A copy for 3s. 2d. (perhaps about £2 or $5 today) was too great a bargain to overlook! Even the burning of copies of Tyndale's New Testament at St. Paul's Cathedral in London in 1530 did not stop the sale; as the importers remarked, the sale of these burned copies was profitable and enabled them to order thousands more!

Tyndale's New Testament was the beginning—it was not a mere translation of Luther, but of the Greek text of Erasmus (1516) ; soon followed his translation of the Pentateuch. On the way to Hamburg to have it printed, his ship was wrecked off the Dutch coast and he lost all his books, his own writings, and manuscript copies, and so had to do the work all over again. But in Hamburg he had the assistance of Miles Coverdale; together they labored in the house of a devout widow, Margaret van Emmerson, "from Easter till December," 1529, and in January of the following year the book was printed. Tyndale's translations had to appear under a pseudonymous imprint; "Hans Lufft, in Marborow in the land of Hesse" was really John Hoochstraten in Antwerp. There is a copy of the New Testament, printed on vellum and presented to Anne Boleyn, in the British Museum. This was a revised issue, "diligently corrected and compared with the Greek," in November 1534. Still another revised edition appeared in 1535; it became the text used in "Matthew's Bible" (1537), the basis of all later "authorized" versions in English.

But in May 1535, Tyndale was again betrayed, this time arrested and imprisoned in the cold damp dungeon of the Castle of Vilvorde, 20 miles south of Antwerp. After months of misery and privation, he was brought out of the dungeon, strangled and burned in the city of Vilvorde on October 6, 1536. His last words were a great cry, "Lord, open the King of England's eyes!"

It is said that nine-tenths of the language of the New Testament in the King James version is derived from Tyndale. Certainly no other translator influenced it half so much. A handsome reprint of Tyndale's New Testament (1534 edition) was published by the Cambridge University Press in 1938, and the reader may enjoy consulting this edition and comparing it with both the authorized Version of 1611 and the Revised Standard Version of 1946. In addition to his New Testament and Pentateuch, Tyndale also left a manuscript translation of the Old Testament from Joshua to the end of Chronicles, based on the Hebrew text, a translation of Jonah, and also the Old Testament passages or portions of Scripture "appointed to be read for the Epistole" according to the use of Sarum (i.e., the ancient rite followed in the Cathedral of Salisbury). His translation of the Beatitudes in Matthew 5:1-12 well illustrates the force and beauty of his style.

THE FYFTH CHAPTER

When he sawe the people/ he went up into a mountaine/ and wen he was sett/ hys disciples cam unto him/ and he opened his mouth/ and taught them sayinge: Blessed are the poore in sprete: for thers is the kyngdom of heven. Blessed are they that mourne: for they shalbe comforted. Blessed are the meke: for they shall inheret* the erthe. Blessed are they which hūger and thurst for rightewesnes: for they shalbe fylled. Blessed are the mercyfull: for they shall obteyne mercy. Blessed are the pure in hert: for they shall se god. Blessed are the maynteyners of peace: for they shalbe called the chyldren of god. Blessed are they which suffre persecucion for rightewesnes sake: for thers is the kingdom of heven. Blessed are ye whē men shall revyle you/ and persecute you/ and shal falsely saye all manner of evle sayings agaynst you for my sake. Reioyce ād be gladde/ for greate is youre rewarde in heven. For so persecuted they the prophetts which were before youre dayes.

The marginal note on "inheret" is as follows:

The worlde thinkethe too possese the erthe/ and to defend there awne/ when they use violence and power: but christ teacheth that the world muste be possessed with mekenes only/ and withoute power and violence.

All these dedes here rehearsed as to norisshe peace/ to shewe

mercy/ to suffre psecuciō/ and so forth/ make not a man
happye and blessed/ nether deserve the rewarde of heven:
but declare and testifie that we are happy and blessede and
that we shall have greate pmociō ī heven. and certyfyeth vs
ī oure hertes that we are goddes sonnes/ & that the holy
goost is in vs. for all good thynges are geven to vs frely of
god for christes blouddes sake ād his merittes.

The special merits and defects of Tyndale's translation
have often been assessed—by no one more judiciously than
by Professor Jacob Isaacs of Queen Mary College, London.[2]
Tyndale's vigor, clarity, euphony, freedom, poetic sense
(alas, that he did not translate the Psalter!), his feeling for Greek and Hebrew idiom, some of which he made
classic in "Bible English"—all this has put later translators
permanently in his debt. It also helps to account for the
sudden shift from official prohibition to official approval of
the English Bible, in the short space of four years. Tyndale's New Testament appeared in 1526. In 1530 Henry
VIII announced—in a backhanded way—that the Bible "shall
be by great learned and catholic persons translated into the
English tongue, if it shall then seem to his grace convenient
so to be": not much of a promise—but a promise, nevertheless, to which in 1534 Archbishop Cranmer insisted upon
holding him.

The editor or translator chosen to undertake this task,
Miles Coverdale, began at once, and succeeded in preparing
his edition for the press within a year. Obviously, he must
have used earlier translations, or had his own all ready to
publish, for the volume appeared in 1535. No claim of au-

[2] See H. W. Robinson, *The Bible in its Ancient and English Versions,*
pp. 156-167.

thority was made for the version, but it was dedicated to the king, who, like King Josiah, "commanded straitly [strictly] that the Law of God should be read and taught unto all the people." This first complete Bible to be printed in English was probably printed in Zürich—not in Holland or in England. Coverdale was a mild, modest man, and claimed for his version only that it was "faithfully and truly translated out of Dutch [i.e., German] and Latin into English" —but even this was too great a confession of dependence upon Lutheran heretics, and later copies read only "faithfully translated into English." But his version—at least of the New Testament—had often been influenced by Luther and Zwingli, in passages where he abandoned Tyndale, and the result was a version more consonant with the growing tendency toward Continental Protestantism which marked the middle decades of the 16th century. The contribution by Coverdale to the making of the English Bible will be clear in a moment, when we consider the "Matthew's Bible." His contribution to the Prayer Book is well known. For the Psalter contained in the Book of Common Prayer is still the Psalter of Miles Coverdale, 76 years older than the King James Version, and never revised, to this day, except for a few slight modifications introduced by the General Convention of the Protestant Episcopal Church in 1928.

In 1537, the year after Tyndale's martyrdom, a Bible was published which was destined to be the basis of all later "authorized" English versions. It was printed in Antwerp, apparently, the cost being provided by two London merchants, Richard Grafton and Edward Whitchurch. It was called the "Matthews" Bible, as the name "Thomas Matthew" follows the dedication. But no one by that name is otherwise known as a Bible scholar, and it is a question whether this was only a pseudonym for John Rogers, the real editor, or the name of an assistant who saw the work through the press. In character, the translation was a continuation of Tyndale's version, and included Tyndale's Pentateuch, New Testament (the final edition, 1535), Coverdale's Apocrypha, Coverdale's translation from Ezra to Malachi, and a new version of Joshua to 2 Chronicles. This last is probably the translation left by Tyndale when he died. It bears all the marks of Tyndale's style and vocabulary. Moreover, the "Matthews" (really Rogers) Bible bore on the title page the statement, "Set forth with the Kinges most gracyous lycence." Evidently Archbishop Cranmer had persuaded Thomas Cromwell to induce the king to allow its publication and use *ad interim*, while the Bishops were preparing a more satisfactory text—which, he added, "I thinke will not be till a day after domesday." At all events, this printing thus became the first Authorized Version of the English Bible. The same privilege was given to Coverdale's Bible, printed that year (1537) in Southwark—the first Bible to be printed in England. One cannot say that Tyndale's dying prayer was answered, "Lord, open the King of England's eyes," for the king was evidently still reluctant and hesitating. But the suddenness of the change, from prohibition to permission, was most remarkable. Evidently a powerful accumulation of public sentiment was pressing for the free and open printing of the English Bible. Even a tyrannous king could not any longer resist the popular demand.

Change was indeed coming rapidly. Despite the Archbishop's pessimism, the so-called "Great Bible" appeared two years later (1539), with a second, revised edition in 1540, containing a preface by Archbishop Cranmer and a clear statement of purpose on the title page: "This is the Byble apoynted to the use of the churches." It was "truly translated after the veryte of the Hebrue and Greke textes, by the dylygent studye of dyverse excellent learned men, expert in the forsayde tonges." The edition of 1540 was a thorough revision by Coverdale of his earlier revision of Matthew—an example of revised versions almost competing! The tendency toward literalism is clearly apparent, with a resulting decline in style from Coverdale's own original euphony and rhythm.

In the New Testament, Erasmus's final edition of the Greek text was used, including many readings which that pioneer had finally adopted from the Complutensian Polyglot of Cardinal Ximenes (1522). In the Old Testament the reliance upon Luther and the Zürich version is less apparent. "The chief fault of the Great Bible is that it is still far from being a direct translation of the Hebrew and Greek, that it is a patchwork of revision, and still relies too much on the authority of the Vulgate." [3]

Meanwhile other versions and revisions appeared. In 1539 Richard Taverner, a layman, issued a revision of the "Matthews" Bible, in smoother English and with closer attention to the Greek, in the New Testament, and the Vulgate, in the Old. During the reign of "bloody" Queen Mary, English Protestant scholars assembled at Geneva in Switzerland and produced (New Testament in 1557, Old

[3] J. Isaacs, in H. W. Robinson, *The Bible in its Ancient and English Versions,* p. 178.

Testament 1560) a still further revision of the current English text, printed in Roman type and divided into verses—but with almost as many notes as text, all in the interest of propaganda for extreme nonconformity and Calvinism. Tyndale's version is still the basis; but the editor, William Whittingham, whose wife was John Calvin's sister, said that the Protestant interpretation of the Bible was made apparent to all readers!

This manner of commending the revisers' theological views proved most distasteful to the Bishops, and in 1566 Archbishop Parker revived Cranmer's dream of an authorized revision to be undertaken by the bishops themselves. The basis was to be the Great Bible already in use in the churches, with no revision beyond what was required by the Hebrew or Greek. The version was to contain "no bitter notes upon any text." But it was "a backward-looking version" (Professor Isaacs), uneven, and in some places close to the Geneva Bible, in others moving in the opposite direction. It aimed at accuracy, but failed to improve its predecessors. For example, Eccl. 11:1 "Cast thy bread upon the waters" became (in words from the Great Bible) "Lay thy bread upon wet faces"; James 4:11 became "Backbite not one another, brethren." The chief importance of the Bishop's Bible lay in the fact that it became, in turn, the basis of the revision of 1611, *the* so-called "Authorized Version," as it has been known ever since.

In 1582 the English Roman Catholics at their College in Rheims produced a translation of the Vulgate designed to offset the "coruptions" contained in the translations by "heretics." Its style was strongly Latinized, and remote from literary English. For example, Eph. 6:12 reads,

"Against the spirituals of wickedness in the celestials." A whole series of transliterations were used—such as Pasche, Azymes, Parasceve, archysynagogue—which have survived in Roman Catholic biblical terminology, and are only now beginning to disappear in the excellent 20th century Catholic translations. At the same time, many excellent renderings are to be found in this New Testament, some of them adopted in the King James Version of 1611 and some also in our Revised Standard Version of 1946. The Douai Old Testament (1610) came too late for use by the King James revisers, and was, moreover, thought to be inferior in quality to the Rheims New Testament, though designed to accompany it and thus complete the Roman Catholic version of the English Bible. Even Bishop Richard Challoner's revision (1749-50) did not succeed in improving it sufficiently, and modern Roman Catholic translations have superseded it.

3. The King James Version

It is said that the King James Version of the Bible resulted from a chance suggestion made by a Puritan, Dr. John Reynolds, at the Hampton Court Conference in January 1604. He proposed that the king should be petitioned to authorize a new translation, as those produced in the reigns of Henry VIII and Edward VI were "corrupt and not answerable to the truth of the original." It was still the "Hebrew veritas" men demanded, as Jerome had sought for it in his translation of the Old Testament!

King James was flattered with the proposal; he had tried his own hand at a "paraphrase" of the Revelation of John and a version of the Psalms in metre. Within a month the project was approved by royal authority and a detailed plan set in motion. It was to include the whole Bible, to be as closely as possible in agreement with the original Hebrew and Greek, and to be the only version used "in all Churches of England in time of Divine Service." Thus the version was "authorized" before it was made, if not after—no record of the actual authorization of the finished version has ever been found! The version was to contain no marginal notes of a theological nature—the bad example of the Geneva version was to be avoided! And the bishops were directed to assemble all the learned men in their dioceses, those having skill in Hebrew and Greek and devoted to "the clearing of any obscurities" or "touching any difficulties or mistakings in the former English translation [the Bishops' Bible], which we have now commanded to be thoroughly viewed and amended"; the scholars were to send their "observations" to the Hebrew Reader in Oxford or Cambridge or to the Dean of Westminster. For the king wanted the translation to be as accurate as possible, and the best that could be made with the help of "all our principal learned men within this our kingdom."

Of the fifty-four learned men appointed by the king for the task of revision, fifty can still be identified. They were not, as a whole, a galaxy of genius, but good, competent, thorough, accurate English scholars. Their workmanship was superb, and the revision has often been described as a literary "miracle." Indeed it was miraculous, especially as the product of a committee, really of three committees;

but it appeared at a time when ordinary spoken English was probably at the height of its development in form, range, versatility, resourcefulness, and rich, musical pronunciation—like St. Augustine's smooth, poetic Latin prose, sonorous and beautiful, with a melody of sound to match the wide variety of his thought and his remarkable depth of feeling. Jacobean English contained all the vast accumulation of language from Chaucer and Wycliffe to the glorious age of Elizabeth I, and now with that of James I added, fired with all the verve and adventure of a turbulent century of ecclesiastical and political reform, of exploration, of war and deliverance, of foreign conquest, of commercial expansion, of creative dramatic expression at home, and of Italian music and song imported from abroad. It was the symphony of a new world, a new age, that men heard ringing in their ears, and hummed as they went about their daily tasks. As far as "timing" went, now was "the fulness of the time" for a truly great version of the Bible to be made; great as the plays of Shakespeare were great, and the Prayer Book of Cranmer, the church music of Tallis, Byrd, and Orlando Gibbons, and the love-lyrics of the Elizabethans. Half the marvel of a miracle is its timing, its local setting in the course of history; and the Jacobean version had all this in its favor. Men who heard and loved the rich cadences of Shakespeare's lines could scarcely have produced a crabbed literal rendering of the Bible. Experts say that the King James Bible is a far greater literary achievement than the original—but the original is not "great literature," except for a few of its eighty books and certain passages in others: Genesis, Job, Psalms, Isaiah, for example, in the Old Testament, or Luke-Acts and Hebrews in the New. Any view of "the Bible as literature" ought to distinguish between the English version and the original Greek and Hebrew; or, in the latter, between what is, consciously or unconsciously, outstanding literature and what is not. For over the whole Bible, in the ancient tongues, is the caption: "These are the oracles of God; they are written in plain language, that men may hearken and obey; they are in the language of every day, so that he who runs may read, and not stumble or fall from the way."

The brief biographies of the fifty identifiable translators —or revisers—may be read in the *Dictionary of National Biography* or elsewhere. On the whole, the record of their lives is "short and simple," the story of scholars, clergymen, and teachers, and not of poets and philosophers or even outstanding theologians. They were formed into three companies—one at Cambridge, one at Oxford, one at Westminster Abbey in London. The last named group, meeting in a library at the Abbey, were charged with the Pentateuch and Joshua to 2 Kings, with "the Epistles of St. Paul and the Canonical Epistles"—presumably the "Catholic Epistles," as we now call them, viz., James, 1-2 Peter, 1-2-3 John, and Jude. Hebrews was included with Paul's epistles. The Cambridge company undertook the Old Testament from 1 Chronicles, "with the rest of the Story," i.e., the history, viz., Ezra, Nehemiah, Daniel, Esther, and the Hagiographa, i.e., Job, Psalms, Proverbs, Chronicles, Ecclesiastes, and also the Apocrypha "with the Prayer of Manasses." It is strange, but no New Testament books were assigned to the Cambridge company. Their assignment was heavy enough in the Old Testament! To the Oxford company were assigned "the former greate Prophets"—meaning the four

Major Prophets, not the "Former Prophets" of Jewish idiom—together with the Lamentations of Jeremiah, and "the twelve lesser Prophets." Oxford also undertook the four Gospels, the Acts of the Apostles, and the Apocalypse.

The rules of procedure of these three companies have been preserved. (1) Their basic text was to be that of "the ordinary Bible read in the Church, commonly called the Bishops' Bible," and it was to be "as little altered as the truth of the original will permit." (2) Proper names, including those of authors of biblical books, were to be retained in the ordinary spelling, and so likewise (3) "the old ecclesiastical words," such as "church" (not "congregation"), and the language was to be kept as close as possible to the traditional norm; (4) words of more than one meaning were to be used in the sense found in "most of the Ancient Fathers," appropriate to the context and consistent with "the analogy of the Faith." (5) The division of chapters found in the Bishops' Bible was to be unaltered, and (6) no marginal notes were to be added, "but only for the explanation of Hebrew or Greek words," or (7) cross-references to relevant passages elsewhere in Scripture. (8) Translations or revisions were to be done first by individuals and then submitted to the whole company for scrutiny and criticism or final approval. (9) As each group of books was finished it was to be submitted to the other two companies, "to be considered of seriously and judiciously, for his Majesty is very careful in this point." (10) If one or the other company, upon this review of a finished book, "doubt or differ upon any place," they were to send word of their objection, and the reasons, and if the original company declined to accept their objection, the difference was to be "compounded at the General Meeting" at the end of the course of revision. (11) In cases of special obscurity the revisers were entitled to request the aid of "any learned man in the land," for his judgment on the correct translation. (12) Every bishop was to send word to the rest of his clergy, urging those "skilful in the tongues" to send their suggestions to the proper company. (13) The directors, or chairmen, of each company were to be the Deans of Westminster and Chester, at London, and the King's Professors ("Regius Professors") of Hebrew and Greek at the two Universities of Oxford and Cambridge. (14) Readings found in five other earlier translations were to be used "when they agree better with the text than the Bishops' Bible," viz., Tyndale's, Matthew's, Coverdale's, Whitchurch's (the Great Bible), Geneva. (15) Finally, a group of "three or four of the most ancient and grave divines, in either of the Universities, not employed in translating . . . [were] to be overseers of the translations as well Hebrew as Greek, for the observation of the 4th rule above specified," viz., the preference of interpretation agreeable to patristic views and consistent with the analogy of the Faith.

It was clear that the version was to be a lectern Bible, to be read in the church. It was to be a revision of the Bishops' Bible, not a new translation, though suggestions might be taken from specified earlier versions—as a matter of fact, they also made use of the Rheims version of the New Testament. It was to be a conservative revision, in the slow, deep, main current of Anglican orthodoxy, loyal to the church fathers, sound in scholarship, free to get light and learning from any source; and it was not to be accompanied by controversial notes on theological interpretation of the kind which had disfigured some earlier versions. Freedom was to be given the reader to add the interpretation—for example, the clergy in their preaching. Above all, it was to be a committee product, and to represent the consensus of the most learned men in the kingdom. King James wanted the "Elizabethan Settlement" to stay settled and not break out into furious controversy and persecution of the kind that had disfigured the preceding century. The long Hampton Court Conference (1604) had been a trial of strength in which it was evident that the opposing forces were fairly well balanced; nothing much was accomplished, save the great major achievement of this discovery of equal powers in opposition, and the futility of any attempt to drive out one or the other party from the Church of England. It is a pity the equilibrium was not more permanent, and that men could not realise, later in the same century, the impossibility of successful revolution and the necessity of mutual toleration, comprehension, and inclusiveness. As Bishop Charles Anderson of Chicago used to say, the genius of Anglicanism consists in its combination of toleration with conviction, of freedom in interpretation with positiveness in maintaining the church's ancient faith.

The revisers were by no means a group of "obscure men"; but they were not very well known to history, great as was their achievement. The actual procedure of the translation has left almost no record, and very little more is known of the final editing and publishing. In fact, there is no manuscript copy of the text as finally delivered to the printer (who was Robert Barker, in London, the publisher of the Bishops' Bible). Years later, in 1660, there appeared a pamphlet entitled "The London Printers Lamentacion," accusing two publishers, John Feild and Henry Hills, of filching and keeping in their own possession the manuscript copy of the King James translation. Nothing more was ever heard of it, and many persons assume that it was destroyed in the Great Fire of London in September 1666.

But another explanation is quite possible. The early printers did not always have "fair copy" to work from. Johann Froben in Basel, for example, set up Erasmus's Greek Testament from the actual manuscripts (three or four in number) which Erasmus used as editor. And since the King James version was no new translation, but both ostensibly and actually a revision of the Bishops', it is not at all unlikely that the printers worked from a copy—or copies—of the earlier book, which had already been published by the same firm. A committee had been appointed to see the version through the press: six men who went daily to Stationers Hall and "in three quarters of a year finished their task," each being paid 30s. a week, the only remuneration any of the revisers ever received for any of their work. These six men took with them to London "three copies of the whole Bible sent from Cambridge, Oxford and Westminster." They were to make a final review of the whole work, and choose "one out of all three, to be committeed to the presse." This is the statement made by Dr. Anthony Walker, one of the revisers, in his life of Dr. John Bois, another reviser, who was one of the six sent to London to supervise the printing. Presumably the three copies were brought into agreement by the committees, and at least one of them contained the final draft. There is in the Bodleian Library at Oxford a copy of the Bishops' Bible in which the margins contain revisions and alterations corresponding closely—but not wholly—with the King James text as printed in 1611. Presumably it is one of those used in the revision, and may have been one of the three taken to London.[4] Such a method of revision would have been far simpler and less laborious, both for the revisers and the printers, than the writing out in long hand of an entirely new draft. Dr. Walker states that John Bois kept notes of the final revision, as it proceeded: "he and he only . . . which notes he kept till his dying day." It is often assumed that these notes have also perished, like the master copy of the revision. But there are good grounds for believing them still extant, at least in part, and we may hope they will be published in due course.

Walker's life of John Bois (1560-1643) is one of the treasures of the Bodleian Library. The manuscript (Tanner 278) is entitled "A Brief description of the Life, and Death of Mr. John Bois, Batchelor in Divinity, and senior Prebendary of the Cathedral Church of Ely. By Anthony Walker, D.D." It is dedicated "To the Right Reverend Father in God Ralph Lord Bishop of Exon" (sic), and contains 60 brief chapters or sections in 12 folios, into which has been inserted a sheet on which is written an account of his books and their disposal after his death. Bois is described as "the chief Greek-lecturer in the Colledge [St. John's, Cambridge] ten years together," often voluntarily "reading" (and lecturing upon) "a Greek book at four of

[4] See the frontispiece to this volume, and the illustration opposite p. 208 in H. W. Robinson, *The Bible in its Ancient and English Versions,* 2nd ed., Oxford, 1954. Some of the marginal changes were adopted, some rejected, and still other changes were made before publication (these latter prove that the copy is not a later adaptation of the Bishops' Bible to the new text of the King James). The master copy given the printer in London must have looked very much like this.

the clock in the morning in his own Chamber, which was frequented by many Fellows" (§ 18). Such early "electives" were evidently rare, even then; for it is said that there were as many candles alight in Bois's bedroom as in all the rest of Cambridge at that hour. But Bois was phenomenal. His father, who was once rector of West Stow near Bury St. Edmunds, had taught him to read Hebrew at the age of six, and he wrote letters in Greek at the age of fifteen. In addition to his college lecturing he was himself rector of a parish, Boxworth, five miles west of Cambridge. His wife—a daughter of the patron of the parish—was not the thrifty kind, and in 1596 poor Bois had to sell his library at a great loss in order to pay the family bills. He nevertheless continued to entrust all financial matters to her judgment, and they took in boarders to meet expenses. When the appointment of the three companies of revisers was made in 1604, Bois was made a member of the Cambridge company (§ 26), and was assigned to work on the Apocrypha—though Walker regretfully acknowledges that he does not know which part. Bois set about the task industriously, visiting his parish from Saturday night to Monday morning and spending the rest of the week at St. John's College. Thus four years were spent in the revision, after which the special committee was chosen and sent to London to see the book through the press. Despite the meticulous threefold chronology of Bois's life, added at the end of the manuscript by another hand—perhaps by someone who questioned the dates given—it is obvious that the "four years" of revision plus "three-quarters of a year" spent in the final review and printing do not begin to fill out the period from 1604 to 1611. Something is clearly wrong with

Walker's dates. Possibly Bois had more tasks assigned him after the first, that on the Apocrypha. Certainly his interests were wider ranging, as is evident from another Bodleian manuscript (Tanner 437), which contains later notes on the Gospels and Acts. This manuscript is entitled *Veteris interpretis cum recensionibus quibusdam in Evangelio secundum Matt.* [*Marc., Luc., etc.*]. These notes were copied by someone else, and the work once belonged to W. Sancroft. A few copies of Bois's notes were published in London in 1655 (one copy is in the British Museum), but the manuscripts, with their frequent changes and erasures, are more interesting.

There is an introduction on Hellenistic Greek in which he quotes the classical scholar, Heinsius: "*Hellenistica lingua nec Graeca est si phrasin spectas, nec Hebraea est si voces spectas!*" (The Hellenistic language is not Greek if you observe the phrasing, nor Hebrew if you note the words!) The first part, on Matthew, is dated April 16, 1619, but the manuscript really begins with *three* pages of notes—as if done sporadically, sometime earlier—on Matt. 2:19 to 25:23, prepared for the printer. In form, the notes anticipate the famous *Novum Testamentum, editio Hellenistica*, of Edward William Grinfield, Oxford, 1843. Matthew was finished August 13, 1619; Mark September 30, 1619; Luke follows, but no date is given for the completion; then John begins, dated on page 1 as on August 30, 1601 (which is obviously wrong), and completed October 13, 1621; Acts was begun October 29, 1621, and completed April 9, 1625. There are a few notes on Romans, but neither these nor the notes on the gospels are of very great importance. They reflect the sound, thorough, workmanlike, pedestrian scholarship of an early seventeenth-century scholar, one of those whose well-trained mind and scholarly instincts produced a far greater literary work, by joint effort, than any one of them could have produced alone. If and when Bois's notes on the final review of the revision appear, we shall have much better evidence of his—and the five other final revisers'—abilities than we possess at present.

Some time during the period of the revision, and perhaps in part accounting for the hiatus between 1608-1610, Bois was engaged in collecting manuscript readings for Sir Henry Savile's noble edition of the works of St. Chrysostom —Savile was another reviser, who at the same time found leisure to edit this great patristic work. Bois travelled extensively on the Continent collating manuscripts and probably sharing in the editorial duties. The eight large volumes of this edition appeared between 1610 and 1613; unfortunately, it is said, Sir Henry died before the final volume appeared, and Bois's only remuneration was one printed copy of the eight volumes! (But Sir Henry Savile died February 19, 1622; obviously the biographer's explanation is at fault.) The work contains notes by Bois scattered over various parts of Chrysostom's works, and Vol. VIII contains two letters addressed by him to the editor. It is said that his wife objected to his overzealous devotion to literature, and burst into his study, one day, with the protest, "I wish I were a book! Then perhaps you would pay some attention to me." A friend of Bois who was present replied, "If you were a book, he might make you an almanac, and change you every year!" "But what *is* this 'Chrysostom,' that takes all your time?" she continued. Upon learning that Chrysostom was a bishop, a saint, and a church father, the lady retracted her remarks and begged the pardon not only of her husband but also of the church father! Today, three and a half centuries later, our sympathies are surely with the unhappy wife of a rather inadequate husband.

The great "Preface of the Translators" which appeared in the 1611 revision is one of the most important and most interesting accounts ever given of the principles and methods guiding a revision of the Bible. It should be read by every serious student of the Scriptures, and especially by all who are interested in the Bible as literature. This Preface was written by Dr. Miles Smith, one of the revisers, a member of the Oxford company who was credited with having "Hebrew at his fingers' ends." It is once more affirmed that the work was a revision, not a completely new book: "Wee never thought from the beginning, that we should neede to make a new Translation, nor yet to make of a bad one a good one . . . but to make a good one better, or out of many good ones, one principall good one, not justly to be excepted against; that hath bene our indeavour, that our marke." This noble *confessio fidei* is echoed in the Preface to the new American *Revised Standard Version*, which was likewise aimed to be a revision, not a new translation, and to follow the main tradition of the English Bible, from Tyndale and Coverdale to the present, including the noble King James Version, in its day the crown and climax of the series. For the King James Version has been, for centuries now, *the* "Authorized Version" of the Bible "appointed to be read in churches," and familiar to countless English-speaking people throughout the world, from early childhood to ripe old age, *the* Bible read from the lectern, studied at school, read and pondered privately and alone, in hardship and sorrow, in joy and release, the companion of all their days. So likewise this is what the Revised Standard Version has striven to provide, in the language of today: "It is a revision which seeks to preserve all that is best in the English Bible as it has been known and used through the years. It is intended for use in public and private worship, not merely for reading and instruction."

4. The Revised Version

The King James Version was produced in an age of Bible translation and revision. As we have seen, it was based upon the Bishops' Bible, as this in turn had been based upon the earlier translations and revisions, all the way back to Tyndale and Coverdale. (No use seems to have been made of the Wycliffite Bible.) It relied upon the most up-to-date scholarship, as is clear from its contents and its marginal notes, which are on the renderings, not on theological matters. Always, the King James Version insists that the most important thing to ascertain is the true meaning of the original Hebrew and Greek. It was not written in archaic language, as a literary performance: its language was not archaic in 1611, but the spoken language of the English people. Its page headings and chapter summaries are still a good guide to the contents; and, unlike some other versions or revisions, these also are factual, not theological or homiletical, for the most part—exceptions will be found in the running interpretation of the Song of Songs as "Concerning Christ and His Church." (Compare the Exhortation in the marriage service, in the Book of Common Prayer.) But the headings and summaries were new, and provide a strong contrast to the earlier ones in the Bishops' Bible, the Geneva New Testament, and others. In the Bishops' Bible, the story in Mark 6, Salome's dance and the beheading of John the Baptist, is entitled: "The inconvenience of dauncing."

Of course, the work is uneven, as was inevitable, since it was produced by three companies working in isolation; and the principle of variety in rendering the same Hebrew or Greek words led to differences which obscured identities of phraseology. This was to be found even in passages where the New Testament quoted the Old, or where one gospel used language identical with that found in another. But, again and again, the final result of the 86 years of experiment and change, from Tyndale to the King James Version, was a version whose accuracy, evenness, and smooth literary style have been a marvel ever since. Take Coverdale's translation of Prov. 3:17, "Her wayes are pleasant wayes and all her paths are peaceable"—a perfectly prosy, unmusical line; and contrast with it the Geneva, "Her wayes are wayes of pleasure and all her paths prosperitie"—still pedestrian, and ending with an economic overtone which reminds us of "Religion and the Rise of Capitalism." But contrast the King James: "Her wayes are wayes of plesantnesse, and all her pathes are peace." It is a perfect rendering of the Masoretic Hebrew text—so perfect that the RSV has left it unaltered—and its final note is that sublime conception which runs throughout the ancient Scripture: *shalōm*, peace, welfare, security, confidence, trust in God; this is the royal way, the pathway of wisdom, righteousness, holiness in the sight of God. This is the true way of life, according to the ancient Hebrew sages. The chapter (VII) on "The Authorized Version and After," by Professor Isaacs, in the late Wheeler Robinson's *The Bible in Its Ancient and English Versions*, contains a whole series of perfect lines, whose antecedents are traced from Tyndale and Coverdale to the King James Version. They are examples of a poetic prose rarely equalled, never excelled, in all the versions of the Bible ever made, before or after.

The version has been altered only very slightly, since its first publication in 1611, chiefly in the more modern spelling of words and in the punctuation. Even the use of italics for words supplied to complete the sense is still retained in modern printings. In the 1611 Bible itself, these words were not printed in italics but in a lower case Roman type, raised slightly above the line. It was obvious that they were supplied to make the English readable, something that the revisers' view of inspiration (i.e., the inspiration of the Hebrew and Greek original) made necessary. It was not long before printers substituted italics for these added words, with the consequence that some readers have assumed that these were the important words and must be strongly emphasized!

It appears that revisions are usually spoken against, beginning with Jerome's revision of the Old Latin Gospels and Psalter. In spite of Pope Damasus' commission, and his approval, there were those who insisted, "The old is better" (Luke 5:39 AV). For a long time, the Geneva Version was preferred in some areas, especially among Puritans; but eventually the King James prevailed. Other versions were made—and have continued to be made to this day. In 1655 it was proposed, in Scotland, that an improved edition of the King James Version should be prepared, beginning with the omission of the Apocrypha, "being merely human," i.e., uninspired writings, and reversing text and margin in more than 800 places! But nothing came of the proposal, nor of one introduced in the Long Parliament to improve the version, since "it is now above forty years since our new translation was finished." Evidently it was believed even then that "time makes ancient good uncouth," and the latest must be the best! Some of the eighteenth-century versions were very bad—pompous, fulsome, rhetorical paraphrases that turned Holy Scripture into a course of lectures on moral philosophy and "rational" religion suiting the taste of Deism and the Enlightenment.

A few advances were made, however, as by Bishop Robert Lowth whose Oxford lectures on "The Sacred Poetry of the Hebrews" (published in 1753) revolutionized the study of the poetical books. It was he who discovered the formal structure of Hebrew poetry, with its three kinds of parallelism (see p. 141), its imagery, its mystical feeling. All interpretation of the Psalms, even of the Prophets, and of the poetical books in general has been changed by Lowth's pioneer researches.

One criticism of the King James Version which is sometimes heard today is its "overpunctuation." True, it contains more commas than we are accustomed to use in modern English. But so does Shakespeare—and, for that matter, the Vulgate, both the Sixtine (1590) and the Clementine (1592) editions. But there is a reason for this flood of commas. As Mr. Charles Laughton explained, when he performed Shakespeare's *King Lear* at Stratford in 1959, the commas make sense when they are observed in reading aloud or in acting. We moderns usually read with our eyes only; but sixteenth-century readers, like ancient readers generally, and especially readers of Shakespeare and the Bible, read aloud. And if one stops, or even merely hesitates, over a comma, the structure of the sentence and the progress and organization of the writer's thought will be clear; moreover, as readers in large churches, cathedrals, halls, and theatres are aware, this "break down" of the sentences avoids both echo and overlapping sounds or elisions which obscure the meaning. Once more, the King James Version was a lectern Bible, meant to be read aloud, and "appointed" —like all preceding versions of the Bible, with few exceptions—"to be read in churches." The same phenomena of punctuation may be found in the Prayer Book, for the same reason, and sometimes subject to the same criticism from modern readers and would-be revisers. Look, once more, at the Exhortation in the Marriage Service, or the long Lesson from 1 Cor. 15 in the Burial Service. To say the least, a proper observance of the punctuation, in oral delivery, prevents the cheap gabbling of the Bible and Prayer Book which are the bane of some unhappy attempts to lead public worship. Robert Browning's "holy mutter of the mass" was no worse than this modern tempo which ruins the conduct of worship and makes it impossible for a congregation to share in it.

But the criticisms which led, in the nineteenth century, to the Revised Version of 1881-85 were concerned, not with punctuation but with the contents, the vocabulary, and the literary style of the King James. Good as it was in its time, the 1611 Bible was a translation based on the medieval text in both Old Testament and New. The Hebrew Old Testament text was that of the early printed editions; the Greek New Testament was the *textus receptus* of Erasmus (1516), Stephanus (1550), and Theodore de Bèze (Beza, 1582). The vocabulary of the King James, its beautiful Elizabethan and Jacobean English, was no longer the language "known and read" by ordinary persons, certainly not by the average schoolboy or schoolgirl, in Victorian days. And its literary style, involving—as we have seen—a variation in rendering of many important (and also many less important) words, irked the Victorian scholars whose minds had been trained in a "literal" rendering of the classics and were now being subjected to the increasing pressure of "scientific" conceptions of learning, with measurable exactitude set up as a standard and norm for all writing and translation. There were also theological conceptions at work in men's minds. There *must* be a standard text of the New Testament; an inspired book *must* have a "neutral" text, to be found in certain manuscripts, uninfluenced by the host of variations found in others. There *must* be a precise theological significance attaching to each theological term used, and every author *must* be self-consistent; St. Paul, for example, must have used every word in his vocabulary in precisely the same way, every time he used it, and each of his ideas must fit exactly into the finished architectural structure of "Paulinism." Otherwise, divine revelation, and the inspiration of Holy Scripture, would not be fully assured. Thus not only were there legitimate complaints of the archaism and obscurity of the old version, but also complaints of the "inconsistencies and errors" which modern scholars wished to remove. Various attempts at improvement of the King James Version, or at more modern translation, were published in the first half of the nineteenth century. One decided advance was the printing of the old version in paragraphs—in this respect reverting to Tyndale and Coverdale; the modern paragraphing of each verse was an innovation of the Geneva Version (1560).

After several decades of discussion and debate, the Upper House of Convocation in the Province of Canterbury, on February 10, 1870, approved a resolution by the Bishop of Winchester, Dr. Samuel Wilberforce, inviting the Province of York to cooperate in the appointment of a committee "to consider and report upon the desirability of revising the erroneous passages in the Authorized Version of the New Testament." With an amendment including the Old Testament, the proposal was adopted—as harmless and tentative a motion as one could conceive! But the Province of York declined to share in any proposal to recast Holy Scripture, and so the movement was undertaken by Canterbury alone. Although at first it was proposed to limit membership of the revision committee to Anglicans, Nonconformists were included and—overstepping York—certain Scottish scholars as well. One Unitarian was named, in addition to several Presbyterians, Methodists, Baptists, and Congregationalists. The majority were from Oxford and Cambridge. An American Committee was formed, under the leadership of Dr. Philip Schaff of Union Theological Seminary, New York, in the expectation that it would cooperate. But the Committee was slow in starting, and the revision was well under way before its first meeting was held (in October 1872), with the result that the Americans could only agree or disagree with changes already made. In the end, the American preferences were listed at the back of the English volume, and were so printed for several years prior to the "American Standard Edition of the Revised Version" in 1901. Even later these preferences continued to appear in English editions of the Revised Version. In general, the Americans were less tolerant of archaism and of traditional ecclesiastical language than the British revisers.

The general principles of the English Revision were clearly stated and adopted at the outset. There were to be two companies, one to revise the Old Testament, the other the New. (1) They were to introduce as few alterations as possible into the text of the Authorized Version, "consistently with faithfulness." (2) The alterations made were to use language found elsewhere in the Authorized Version or in the earlier English versions. (3) Each company was to go over the whole text twice, once provisionally, again finally. (4) The text adopted must have preponderant support, and if it disagreed with the text translated in 1611 a marginal note must give the reason. (5) A simple majority could decide the rendering the first time; but a two-thirds majority was to be required for final adoption. (6) Debated renderings must be deferred for final action until the next meeting, if a third of those present requested it. (7) Chapter headings, page headings, paragraphing, punctuation, and italics were to be revised where necessary. (8) When considered desirable, the advice of theologians, scholars, and literary men was to be invited.

The Old Testament company met in the Chapter Library at Westminster Abbey, the New Testament company in the Jerusalem Chamber. The Old Testament revision took fourteen years, the New Testament ten and a half. The Revised New Testament appeared in 1881, the Old Testament in 1885. The publication was entrusted to the University Presses at Oxford and Cambridge, who were given exclusive rights for fourteen years, during which time they were to contribute £20,000 towards the expenses of the revision. It was for this reason that the American Committee did not produce their edition until later. When the fourteen years were up, in 1899, they assembled and prepared the "American Standard Edition" (not the "American Revision," as it is often called). This was published in 1901 by Thomas Nelson and Sons in New York.

The welcome reception given the English Revised Version was widespread. Two American newspapers, the Chicago *Times* and the Chicago *Tribune*, had the whole New Testament sent them (partly by telegraph!) and published it in special Sunday supplements.[5] People welcomed the new arrangement of the text in paragraphs, not broken up into separate verses, and poetry printed "as poetry"; the careful reference to manuscript or other authority for new readings; the promise of "faithfulness" and consistency in rendering the same word in the same way—a valuable feature for people arguing in support of verbal inspiration or resting their theological views upon "a literal Bible"—all these factors appealed strongly to multitudes of Bible readers, new and old. At the same time the tone of the Version was almost identical with that of the familiar "Authorized." Few persons realized that it was even more archaic, that it had introduced even older words, which were still in use, in place of archaic and obscure ones in the King

[5] Rogation Sunday, May 22, 1881.

James rendering. But expressions like "his," for impersonal subjects, were replaced by "its," and just enough modern language was introduced to justify its date, 1881 or 1885. Its close relation to the Greek text of Westcott and Hort, in the New Testament, was a further guarantee of accuracy and trustworthiness. This confidence was further increased when new editions of the Greek New Testament began to appear, bearing subtitles or stating in their prefaces that the text was that of the revisers.

But the reception accorded the Revision was not like that which hailed the "Authorized" in 1611. Not only were there bitter attacks upon it from ultraconservatives, but the popular response was ephemeral, and it never became the favorite version of the majority of English-speaking Christians. For one thing, it was still archaic. For another, it was too literal to be a good translation—at least in the New Testament; the Old Testament translators, as often, allowed themselves more freedom in the rendering of the highly imaginative, poetic, figurative or symbolic language of the prophets and psalmists. They were translating poetry. And in the Old Testament the King James revision could scarcely be improved; certainly the Masoretic Hebrew text had not changed in 270 years, as the commonly used Greek text of the New Testament had changed. Finally, the principle of "faithfulness," which prevailed especially in the New Testament company, where it was urged and defended constantly by Dr. Joseph Lightfoot, afterwards (January 1879) Bishop of Durham, resulted not only in a uniformity of rendering which resembled that of a schoolboy's "pony" but also in an absurd, unidiomatic order of English words designed to conform to "the order of the

Greek." The idea was to give such a rendering as might with the greatest ease be slipped back into the original, in a word-for-word substitution, by anyone who could use a Greek dictionary, whether he could read the Greek language or not. It is almost as bad as Aquila's literal "translation" of the Old Testament into second-century Greek: no wonder the Hellenistic Jews gave it up! And no wonder the Revised Version of the English Bible has never won the warm approval and affection so long enjoyed by the King James. Once more, the outlook and ethos of the age had influenced the translation of the Bible, in this case the profound, ubiquitous, opulent conservatism of the Victorian era.

V.

THE BIBLE
TODAY

1. The New Translations

FROM 1611 to 1870 the changes made in the "Authorized" Version were of only minor importance, chiefly matters of punctuation, spelling, and typography. But the Revised Version of 1881-85 was a major change which troubled many readers and proved wholly unacceptable to some; it never won acceptance by the majority of Bible readers, and to this day most Bibles read at public worship or in private study or devotional meditation are the King James. The most magnificent handset Bible of modern times, the famous edition composed by Bruce Rogers, is the King James "Authorized" Bible. Many Christians cling to it as inspired and therefore sacred. The frequent reference to a "St. James Bible" is more than a joke or a slip of the tongue. As St. Augustine and others viewed the Septuagint as inspired, and as some Roman Catholics view the Vulgate, so many Protestants think of the traditional English text —which no one should attempt to alter. Mr. William Collins, the British publisher, has said, "When the first traveller takes a Bible to the moon, you may be sure it will be a copy of the Authorized Version." Perhaps it will off-set the Soviet insignia landed there in advance, by rocket! But is this the real purpose of the publication, or the reading, of the Bible? It is like Bibles buried in cornerstones, or kept in courtrooms where oaths are administered!

The critics of the King James Version refer to its mellow and mellifluous cadences, even in lines that call for harsh broken tones. For example, "Except ye repent, ye shall all likewise perish" (Luke 13:3, 5). Or the Cry of Dereliction, "My God, my God, why hast thou forsaken me?" (Mark 15:34). Or the screaming words of the demoniac in Capernaum, "Let us alone; what have we to do with thee, thou Jesus of Nazareth? art thou come to destroy us? I know thee who thou art, the Holy One of God" (Mark 1:24). The tone is as calm as the reply of Jesus that follows: "Hold thy peace, and come out of him." Of course, the language is supported by the original; this is what the Greek *says*. But the tone is relaxed, "churchy," almost soporific. Moreover, the "Authorized" Version is so familiar to most Bible readers that they are lulled rather than stirred by it. One would never suspect the King James Bible of containing "dynamite," as James Russell Lowell said of the Sermon on the Mount. And this relaxed tone is a quality one does not want —or should not seek for—in the Bible; it is no soft, soothing lullaby but a shout of warning. In many a passage—in all parts of both Old Testament and New—it is meant to "stab our spirits broad awake" and keep them so, through the perilous times that are upon us. The somnolent mellifluity of the old version is only too compatible with the one-sided presentation of Christian ethics and moral theology one often hears today, for which the cardinal virtues have become humility and patience. But there are intolerable evils in our world, and both Bible and Prayer Book command us to "make no peace with oppression" (*Book of Common Prayer*, p. 44). Half the earth is still "full of darkness and cruel habitations," and no Christian or Jew or even humanist can close his eyes to the horrible conditions which doom whole generations to a brutish, subnormal way of life, and whole families to hunger, filth, and vice. Certainly the Bible—as well as the Prayer Book—should be set free to speak clearly and unmistakably to our own time, and deliver its message, which is nothing less than God's word to all men everywhere, "beginning with us," as we say in the well-known prayer!

To revert once more to Eduard Meyer's insistence upon the "anthropological" or sociological background of history, it was probably impossible in the 1870's to produce a version which should be looking ahead rather than backward. The lush times of Queen Victoria's middle years, the seeming-safe passage beyond the dark era of the Industrial Revolution, the Corn Laws, factory riots at home and revolutions abroad, encouraged a self-assured outlook in theology and religious life. A little rewriting here and there, the substitution of words still well understood, but really "good old" Jacobean terms found in the literature of England's Silver Age, a slight change in word-order to correspond more closely to that of the original Greek or Hebrew, but retaining the hallowed, time-honored Bible language, "thee, thou, and thy"—this was all that was needed! No wonder the Revised Version, especially in its American edition, was not a great success. And no wonder that two major projects for revision or retranslation have been undertaken in our time. The first is the American Revised Standard Version of 1946-52-57; the second is the new English translation, promised for 1961.

Of course, Bible translation is an endless process, as languages change, as additional copies of ancient manuscripts continue to turn up, and as scholars come to know and understand the ancient languages better. Our age is conspicuously an age of Bible translation and revision, like the sixteenth century, the period beginning with Tyndale and ending with King James. The University of Chicago Professor Richard G. Moulton's *Modern Readers' Bible* (1907-26) was an early example, in this century, of the "literary" study of the Bible, especially of its poetic and dramatic forms. It made use of the Revised Version, slightly amended by the incorporation of marginal readings in the text. A wholly fresh American rendering of the New Testament appeared in 1898-1901, with the title, *The Twentieth Century New Testament*. It was based on Westcott and Hort's Greek text, with prefaces and paragraph headings. But it was produced by an anonymous committee, which was —certainly in our century—a handicap rather than an advantage. Dr. Richard Francis Weymouth's *New Testament in Modern Speech* appeared in 1903, a version based upon his own edition of the Greek text, entitled *The Resultant Greek Testament* (1886), in which he averaged the best modern editions.

More widely read was Dr. James Moffatt's *The New Testament: a New Translation* (1913), followed eventually by *The Old Testament* (1924) and a revision of the whole (in 1935). He was at work in his study at Union Theological Seminary on a translation of the Apocrypha at the time of his death (in 1944). He had reached the famous passage in Wisdom 3, "The souls of the righteous are in the hand of God, and no torment will ever touch them," when he laid down his pen for the last time. Moffatt's version is more popular, even more colloquial than most others; at the same time it achieves a high level of literary beauty in many passages—especially in Job, in the gospels, and in Paul. The familiar rebuke in the gospel, "Why are you afraid? Have you no faith?" (Mark 4:40), becomes "O men, why don't you trust him?" Here Moffatt the pastor and preacher becomes Moffatt the scholar and exegete—or *vice versa!* Many have found his translation of the obscure Pauline epistles a revelation of clarity and penetration of thought. Some readers, used to the smooth mellifluity of the King James, thought Moffatt's renderings "undignified." But there was a stern Scot's sense of reality running through it all, and it remains one of the great translations. Unfortunately, the New Testament was based upon Baron Hermann Von Soden's Greek text, which in 1913 was thought to be epoch-making, but has since proved extremely disappointing. However, the peculiarities of Von Soden's text, so far as they are carried over into Moffatt's translation, are few and far between, and are easily corrected.

In 1923, Professor Edgar J. Goodspeed of the University of Chicago published *The New Testament: an American Translation.* It was based on the Greek text of Westcott and

Hort, and was done in ordinary everyday American speech —some called it "journalistic" or "newspaper English." To this charge Dr. Goodspeed replied by pointing out the fact that the Greek New Testament was written in *Koinē* or "common" Greek, the language of every day, of first-century laborers and artisans, slaves and tradesmen, not the polished "Atticist" Greek affected by the intelligentsia. So effective was Goodspeed's thesis and its demonstration that in 1935 the University of Chicago Press followed his translation with one of the Old Testament, by Professors J. M. P. Smith, A. R. Gordon, T. J. Meek, and Leroy Waterman. In 1938, Dr. Goodspeed added a translation of the Apocrypha, and the whole Bible appeared soon after under the title, *The Complete Bible: an American Translation* (1939). Unfortunately, the textual notes printed in the first edition of the Old Testament had to be omitted from the final edition. They are important, not only for a study of the translation but for any study of the Old Testament text. The Massoretic Hebrew text was somewhat freely handled by the translators.

Another important modern version is *The Holy Scriptures According to the Massoretic Text: a New Translation*, edited by Professor Max Margolis and a group of American Jewish scholars, and published by the Jewish Publication Society (Philadelphia, 1917). It is a beautiful, dignified rendering of the sacred text, often quoted by scholars, both Jewish and Christian. At the present time still another Jewish version is in progress, somewhat more modern in tone and diction, and less under the influence of the traditional "Bible" English.

Among Roman Catholic versions, mention must be made

of *The Westminster Version of the Sacred Scriptures* by Fathers Cuthbert Lattey and Joseph Keating (begun in 1913). The Old Testament is based on the Hebrew text, and the general character is that of "Biblical" English. A further revision of Bishop Challoner's revision (1749-50) of the Rheims-Douai Bible appeared in 1941, and in 1954 *The New Testament Rendered from the Original Greek* by Fathers James A. Kleist and Joseph Lilly. A magnificent translation by an American classicist, Fr. Francis A. Spencer, was published in 1937. At present still another version of the Old Testament is under way (begun in 1952). It is based upon the Hebrew text. The popular English New Testament issued by the Confraternity of Christian Doctrine, published by the St. Anthony's Guild Press, and available even outside the book shops, is one of the very best of modern versions. It is based upon the Vulgate; a revision, based upon the Greek, is said to be in preparation. There are also excellent modern translations, by Roman Catholic scholars, in French and German and many other languages; and there are also many translations in various languages by Protestants.

One of the most accurate, readable, and most beautifully printed is the *Jerusalem Bible*, under the general editorship of Fr. R. de Vaux, O.P., Director of the Dominican School of Biblical Studies in Jerusalem; Fr. P. Benoit, O.P., Professor there; Msgr. L. Cerfaux of the University of Louvain; Canon E. Osty, P.S.S., of the Catholic Institute in Paris; Fr. P. Auvray, of the Oratory; Professor E. Gilson, of the French Academy; Professor H.-I. Marrou, Professor at the Sorbonne; M. Gabriel Marcel, member of the Institute; Michel Carrouges; and three departed members: A. Robert,

P.S.S., J. Huby, S.J., and Albert Béguin. In addition to the excellent translation, the text is furnished with good brief introductions, adequate marginal references, and first-class footnotes. There are also chronological and genealogical tables, and even an index to the footnotes. Everything possible has been done to make the reading of Holy Scripture easy and interesting for the "common reader." The work is a model of what should be done to make the Bible interesting and attractive to the present generation. An unusual amount of the biblical text is printed as poetry, bringing out the poetic structure of the original.

A beautiful translation of the Latin Vulgate was made by the late Msgr. Ronald Knox (New Testament in 1945, Old Testament in 1949). His English is free and more or less modern, but still shows traces of the old King James Version in which he was reared.[1] With his immense clarity of mind, his frankness and honesty of purpose, Knox acknowledged that there are passages where the Vulgate is quite meaningless, or obviously wrong (in conflict with the context); in such places he turned to the Hebrew, and gave a literal translation of the Vulgate in a footnote.

There are other recent "translations" which are really paraphrases—useful, clear, and "making many rich," but not in the line of descent from the classic translations of the past. One such is the admirable series of *New Testament Letters* by Bishop J. W. C. Wand (1949) and the *Letters to Young Churches* by J. B. Phillips (1947), later followed

---

[1] One may compare Knox's translation of Hebrews 1:1-9 with others, from Tyndale to the RSV, in Appendix II to Sir Frederic Kenyon's *Our Bible and the Ancient Manuscripts,* new ed. by A. W. Adams, London, 1958.

by a translation of the Gospels (1952) and *The Young Church in Action*, i.e., the Book of Acts (1955). The whole New Testament is now available in this version (1958). Dr. E. V. Rieu has translated the Gospels and Acts for the Penguin Series, of which he is editor—he has also translated Homer, both the *Iliad* and the *Odyssey*, for this series. *The New Testament: a New Translation in Plain English* by C. K. Williams appeared in 1952. A curious work is *The Bible in Basic English* (1949), in a vocabulary of 850 words plus 50 special biblical words and 100 others to make a total of 1000. "Basic English" is a simplified language for those who are beginning to learn English, and who find the Bible too rich in vocabulary—though the King James has a moderate range.[2] Many readers have misunderstood the purpose of the "reduced" vocabulary. It is not "basic" philologically, but is a *B*ritish-*A*merican *S*cientific *I*nternational *C*ommercial language, completely artificial and utilitarian. For example, "to cast a stone" becomes "put a stone"—which sounds like the old-fashioned "shot-put" on the athletic fields of American colleges.

The late Charles C. Torrey of Yale University published (in 1933; revised in 1947) a translation of the Gospels, in support of his theory of Aramaic originals underlying the Gospels, Acts 1—12, and the Apocalypse. Aside from a few places where he believed a hypothetical reconstruction of this Aramaic basis would make clearer the meaning of the Greek, there is little in the translation to mark it off from others. But most of the suspected passages are clear enough in

[2] Using Cruden's *Concordance* and omitting the proper nouns and close derivatives, it is estimated that the King James vocabulary totals about 4700 words.

Greek, and the theory as a whole has not won wide acceptance.[3] A similar work has been produced by George Lamsa,
as a translation from the original Aramaic in which Jesus
taught his disciples. But this original Aramaic does not survive in any New Testament. The translation is really based
on the later Syriac, which belongs to the same language-
family, but is not identical with the Western Aramaic spoken
in Galilee in the opening years of the first century.[4] It
adopts some renderings that are very questionable. For
example, in the saying, "It is easier for a camel to go through
the eye of a needle than for a rich man to enter the kingdom
of God" (Mark 10:25, Luke 18:25, Matt. 19:24), "camel"
becomes "a rope" or "hawser" (*kamilon* for *kamēlon*) in a
few ancient manuscripts and versions, e.g., the Old Georgian
and the Armenian. But how much easier or more natural
would it be to thread a needle with a ship's hawser than to
lead a camel through the eye? The language is that of
Jewish hyperbole: scholars said that the erudite teachers at
Pumbeditha made elephants perform this trick, as the later
Schoolmen described an abstruse metaphysical theorem as an
attempt to determine "how many angels could dance on the
point of a needle." It is a popular modern idea that beside
the large city-gate, in ancient Palestine, was a low narrow
postern, through which latecomers could enter after the main

---

[3] He also translated the Apocrypha (1946), Revelation (1958), Chronicles
and Ezra (1954).

[4] *The Four Gospels according to the Eastern Version,* translated from
the Aramaic by George M. Lamsa (Philadelphia: Holman, 1933); this is
now included in his larger work, *The Holy Bible, Translated from the
Ancient Eastern Manuscripts: Containing the Old and New Testaments,
Translated from the Peshitta, the Authorized Bible of the Church of the
East* (*ibidem,* 1957).

gate had been closed for the night. But there is no evidence for this interpretation any earlier than the mid-nineteenth century, when romantic exegetes invented the name, "The Needle's Eye Gate." A city with a small gate beside the big one would scarcely meet "security requirements" in the days of stone walls and fortifications. Moreover, no camel or other quadruped, especially loaded with freight, could get down on its knees and crawl, in the way described by the nineteenth-century homiletical expositors as an example to the rich man, who must humble himself and pray! Dogs can "hunch along," but not cows, horses, or camels. The substitution of "rope" for "camel" in two old Oriental versions is clearly a mistake, not a survival of the original reading.

2. The Revised Standard Version

It was largely because of the failure of the Revised Version of 1881-85 and 1901 that the International Council of Religious Education (now a constituent part of the National Council of Churches of Christ in the United States of America) decided to undertake a new revision. This decision was reached in 1928, when the copyright of the 1901 "American Standard Edition" of the Revised Version expired. The purpose of the new revision was to be as follows:

To embody the best results of modern scholarship as to the meaning of the Scriptures, and express this meaning in English diction which is designed for use in public and private worship and preserve those qualities which have given to the King James Version a supreme place in English literature. We therefore define the task of the American Standard Bible Committee to be that of revision of the present American Standard Bible in the light of the results of modern scholarship, this revision to be designed for use in public and private worship and to be in the direction of the simple, classic English style of the King James Version.

This emphasis, from the outset, upon the use of the version in public worship placed it directly in line with the earlier "authorized" versions—the Great Bible, the Bishops' Bible, the King James—and indeed with the "great Bibles" of antiquity, the Hebrew Bible, the Aramaic Targums, the Greek, Latin, and Syriac Bibles and also the old ecclesiastical versions subsidiary to them—the Coptic, Armenian, Georgian, Gothic, and still others, including Medieval and Reformation Bibles, the German, the French, and many besides.

The International Council also stressed the importance of a clear, accurate, modern revision for use in religious education. It was evident, by 1928, that the Revised Version, including its American edition of 1901, was too literal to be good English or even a good translation—it was better suited to be "an interlinear translation for incompetent school-boys," as the *Edinburgh Review* had said as early as July 1881! It was also clear that the advances in scholarship in the course of nearly sixty years had rendered imperative a new revision: far better editions of the Bible, both Old Testament and New, and also the Apocrypha, were now available, thanks to newly discovered manuscripts, new dictionaries and grammars based on the flood of papyrus documents edited at the end of the nineteenth and the beginning of the twentieth centuries. These discoveries mostly came after the Revised Version was finished. Finally, the Council insisted,

> In the Bible we have not merely a historical document and a classic of English literature, but the Word of God. And the Bible carries its full message, not to those who regard it simply as a heritage of the past or praise its literary style, but to those who read it that they may discern and understand God's Word to men. That Word must not be hidden in ancient phrases which have changed or lost their meaning; it must stand forth in language that is direct and clear and meaningful to the people of today.

The Council chose and appointed a group of scholars, sixteen in number, to be responsible for the new revision. Forty denominations were represented in the Council, and the choice of the actual revisers was made in consultation with denominational authorities. In addition to the revisers, fifty representatives of cooperating denominations were to act as an Advisory Board, and review the work either as it progressed or before publication. The new revision is obviously an "authorized" version in the full sense, as both its preparation and its publication were authorized by the National Council of Churches of Christ in the United States of America. It is also recommended by the Canadian Council of Churches, Department of Christian Education; and it is already widely approved and in general use throughout the English-speaking world.

Six of the original sixteen members appointed in 1929-31 formed the nucleus of the larger group of twenty-two appointed in 1937, when the revision got fully under way. These six were the following:

Dean Luther A. Weigle, Yale University, 1929, Old Testament and New Testament, Chairman;

James Moffatt, Union Theological Seminary, 1930 (died 1944), Old Testament and New Testament, Executive Secretary;

Julius A. Bewer, Union Theological Seminary, 1930 (died 1953), Old Testament;

Henry J. Cadbury, Harvard University, 1930, New Testament;

Edgar J. Goodspeed, University of Chicago, 1930, New Testament;

William R. Taylor, University of Toronto, 1931 (died 1951), Old Testament.

To these members of the original Committee were now added the following sixteen:

Walter Russell Bowie, Union Theological Seminary, 1937, New Testament;

George Dahl, Yale University, 1937, Old Testament;

Frederick C. Grant, Union Theological Seminary, 1937, New Testament;

William A. Irwin, University of Chicago, 1937, Old Testament;

Willard L. Sperry, Harvard University, 1937 (died 1954), Old Testament;

Leroy Waterman, University of Michigan, 1937, Old Testament;

Millar Burrows, Yale University, 1938, Old Testament and New Testament;

- Clarence T. Craig, Drew Theological Seminary, 1938 (died 1953), New Testament;
- Abdel R. Wentz, Lutheran Theological Seminary, Gettysburg, 1938, New Testament;
- Kyle M. Yates, Southern Baptist Theological Seminary, 1938, Old Testament;
- William F. Albright, The Johns Hopkins University, 1945, Old Testament;
- J. Philip Hyatt, Vanderbilt University, 1945, Old Testament;
- Herbert G. May, Oberlin Graduate School of Theology, 1945, Old Testament;
- James Muilenburg, Union Theological Seminary, 1945, Old Testament;
- Harry M. Orlinsky, Jewish Institute of Religion, New York, 1945, Old Testament;
- Fleming James, University of the South, 1947 (died 1959), Executive Secretary of the Old Testament Section.

Still others were added, and a special committee was appointed in 1953 to revise the Apocrypha (published in 1957). This addition, designed to "complete" the RSV Bible, was made at the request of the General Convention of the Protestant Episcopal Church in October 1952. Dean Weigle continued as Chairman; the other members of the Committee were Professors Millar Burrows of Yale University, Henry Cadbury of Harvard University, Clarence T. Craig of Drew Theological Seminary, Floyd V. Filson of McCormick Theological Seminary, Frederick C. Grant of Union Theological Seminary, Bruce M. Metzger of Princeton Theological Seminary, Robert H. Pfeiffer of Harvard University (died 1957), Allen P. Wikgren of the University of Chicago. Further, four members of the National Council served *ex officio:* J. Carter Swaim, Roy G. Ross, Paul C. Payne, and Gerald E. Knoff.

In addition to the Prefaces to the New Testament (1946) and the Old Testament (1952)—and also to the two combined in 1952—which set forth the principles and methods followed by the Revision Committee, there are two pamphlets which provide an "Introduction to the RSV." These —as well as the Prefaces—should be read by every serious student of the new revision. The one on the New Testament contains chapters on the Revision of the English Bible; the King James and the American Standard Versions of the New Testament; the Semitic Background of the New Testament; the Making of the New Testament, Greek and Roman Factors; the Greek Text of the New Testament; the Vocabulary and Grammar of New Testament Greek; the English of the Revised Standard Version of the New Testament; the Use of the New Testament in Worship; the New Testament and the Word of God. The volume on the Old Testament contains chapters on the Method and Procedure of the Revision; the Authorized Revisions of the King James Version; the Hebrew Text and the Ancient Versions of the Old Testament; the Language of the Old Testament; the Geography of the Old Testament and the RSV; Archaeology and the Translation of the Old Testament; the Style and Vocabulary of the RSV Old Testament; the Poetry of the Old Testament; the Wisdom Literature of the Old Testament; Preaching Values of the RSV, the Prophets; the Use of the Old Testament in Worship; Some Misleading Words in the King James Version.

There is also a brief Preface to the Apocrypha (1957) which deserves study. In lieu of an official "Introduction" by members of the Committee, it is enough to refer to the admirable recent books on the Apocrypha by four of the revisers, Edgar J. Goodspeed, Robert H. Pfeiffer, Bruce M. Metzger, and Floyd V. Filson.[4a] It is generally agreed that "modern historical interest . . . is putting the Apocrypha in their true place as significant documents of a most important era in religious history." Anglicans, especially, are interested in this recovery of books which were quite arbitrarily omitted from the Bible, chiefly by publishers, early in the nineteenth century,[5] on the basis of opposition from Puritans who insisted they were "no part of the Canon of Scripture," not being of divine inspiration, and "therefore . . . of no authority in the Church of God, nor to be otherwise approved, or made use of, than other human writings" (see the *Westminster Confession*, 1648). The Anglican or Episcopal Church has always held, with St. Jerome, that these fourteen (or fifteen) books "are to be read for example of life, and instruction of manners," but not "to establish any doctrine." The liturgical use of certain books of the Apocrypha in the Anglican Church, the Lutheran, and even the Swiss Calvinist, has kept them before Protestants ever since the Reformation. In the Greek and Roman Churches, which use the Septuagint and the Vulgate respectively, they have been questioned, but never rejected. A generation aroused to the importance of the period "between the Testaments" by such writings as *The Apocrypha and Pseudepigrapha of the Old Testament*, published in two huge volumes by R. H. Charles in 1913, and aware of the implications of the newly

[4a] See titles in the bibliography at the end of this volume.

[5] In 1827, under pressure from certain of their constituents, the American and British Bible Societies stopped printing the Apocrypha.

discovered (1947 and following) Dead Sea Scrolls, is not likely to ignore the Apocrypha any longer. It may be said that whereas the Revised Version Apocrypha, added in 1894, was based upon a somewhat sketchy review of the King James Version, the new RSV Apocrypha rests upon just as thorough and searching an examination of the linguistic, textual, and historical evidence as the rest of the RSV. All the available ancient versions were consulted; all the great printed editions; all the standard modern commentaries and some of the ancient. No more thorough English edition has ever been prepared, certainly none of those in the sixteenth century or the King James itself.

Of the two earlier parts, the New Testament and the Old, the words of a most eminent scholar, palaeographer, and editor of biblical and classical texts may be quoted. After describing the production of the Revised Standard Version, the late Sir Frederic Kenyon summed it up as follows:

[It has] met with immense success not only in America but also in England. The principles on which the revision was carried through prevented any very radical departure from traditional Biblical usage, while at the same time there is a great gain in clarity and directness of expression. Again, it partakes much more of the nature of an 'authorized version' since, in contrast to the numerous attempts at revision or translation by individuals, it is known to be the work of a body of scholars eminent in their own right as well as representative of the different Churches. In all respects it stands on its own merits as a most important landmark in the history of the English Bible.[6]

[6] *Our Bible and the Ancient Manuscripts,* new edition 1958, p. 329.

Such commendation by one of the world's foremost authorities on the history of the Bible and its translations is most gratifying to all who have had any part, large or small, in the production of the Revised Standard Version.

3. The New English Translation

Even before World War II, when the copyrights of the English Revised Version were running out, plans for a new revision were being considered: the Revised Version was proving unsatisfactory even in England. After the war, the Scottish Church, led by the Presbytery of Stirling and Dunblane, took up the idea energetically, insisting upon a completely new and modern translation. In 1947 a Joint Committee was appointed (*a*) to represent the Established Churches of England (Anglican) and Scotland (Presbyterian), the Free Churches in Great Britain, the University Presses of Oxford and Cambridge, and other interested bodies; and (*b*) to undertake a new translation of the entire Bible, including the Apocrypha.

The first Chairman of this Joint Committee was Dr. J. W. Hunkin, Bishop of Truro; following his death in 1950, the Bishop of Durham, now Bishop of Winchester, Dr. A. T. P. Williams, became Chairman. The General Director of the whole project is Professor Charles H. Dodd, who is known throughout the world as a biblical scholar of the very first rank; he is also Convener of the New Testament Panel of revisers. Professor G. R. Driver, the eminent authority on Semitic languages, is Convener of the Old Testament Panel. Professor George D. Kilpatrick is Convener of the Panel dealing with the Apocrypha; he is the well-known editor of the new British and Foreign Bible Society edition of the Greek New Testament which is taking the place of the old original edition by Eberhard Nestle (1898). There is also a Literary Panel, headed by the Bishop of Winchester, devoting its attention to the English style of the version, which is to be in modern "timeless" English, without pedantry or "hallowed associations," and speak to the present generation as vividly and forcefully as the Bible originally spoke to its contemporaries.

The members of the Panels are as follows.

Old Testament: Professor G. R. Driver, Oxford University, Convener, following the lamented death of Professor T. H. Robinson; Professors H. H. Rowley of Manchester; N. W. Porteous of Edinburgh; C. R. North, Bangor; B. J. Roberts, Menai Bridge, Anglesey; W. D. McHardy, Oxford; A. R. Johnson, Cardiff; Dean Cuthbert A. Simpson, Christ Church, Oxford; the Rev. L. H. Brockington, Oxford.

New Testament: Professors C. H. Dodd, Cambridge University (now Oxford), Convener; George S. Duncan (deceased); T. W. Manson (deceased); R. V. G. Tasker, Surbiton, Surrey; C. F. D. Moule, Cambridge; G. D. Kilpatrick, Oxford; J. A. T. Robinson, Cambridge (now Bishop of Woolwich); Geoffrey M. Styler, Cambridge.

The Apocrypha: Professors G. D. Kilpatrick, Oxford, Convener; W. D. McHardy, Oxford; J. R. Porter, Oxford; W. H. Cadman, Oxford; J. Y. Campbell, Cambridge.

The Literary Panel: The Bishop of Winchester, Dr. A. T. P. Williams, Convener; the Dean of York; the Ven. Adam Fox,

Westminster Abbey; Professors W. F. Oakeshott, Oxford; R. A. B. Mynors, Oxford; Basil Willey, Cambridge; A. L. P. Norrington, Oxford.

There are also additional translators, not on the Panels, as follows:

Old Testament: Principal Norman Snaith, Leeds; Professor John Mauchline, Glasgow. *Apocrypha:* Professor Matthew Black, St. Andrews; G. W. Anderson, Birmingham; the Archbishop of Armagh, Ireland.

The reasons for undertaking an entirely new translation, rather than (as in the case of the RSV) a revision of the traditional English Version, are as follows: (1) There are now many persons who no longer have any real contact with the churches or with organized religion or with public worship. For these persons the King James Bible has no associations whatsoever, sacred or other. Many of them are intelligent enough to grasp the meaning of Scripture and its message if only the Bible is presented to them in a language ordinary persons of today can understand. The language of 1611, and of modern versions based thereon, is quite unintelligible. It is obvious from this statement that the "liturgical" purpose and use—so prominent hitherto, from the days of Ezra and certainly throughout most of Christian history, and clearly an essential element in the tradition of the English Bible hitherto, including the RSV—are not included in its motivation. But the *missionary* purpose of the translation, its intended use in "home" missions, is wholly admirable. (2) There are "modern" schools where the Bible is read— but not as Jacobean literature. (3) There are multitudes of people (not only in Great Britain) to whom the Authorized version is "so familiar that they are lulled rather than aroused by its phrases, but who would be more likely to respond to the stimulus of a new and contemporary version which will break through the barrier of familiarity." This is why it is hoped thus to achieve a "timeless" English, free from both archaism and ephemeral modernism, a language which will speak to this generation with the same power as that with which the original spoke in ancient times.

Thus the English-speaking world will have two modern "authorized" versions: the American, strangely enough, in the direct line of descent from the King James; and the British, striking out a new path. Certainly there is room for both, on both sides of the Atlantic! May each complement and support the other, and may both together serve the purposes of divine worship, of religious instruction, of private edification, and the zealous missionary proclamation of God's everlasting message to all mankind!

VI.

PRINCIPLES

AND

PROBLEMS

1. The Text

THE first duty of every translator is to adop the most accurate and reliable text of the work before him— unless he is to translate an autograph, i.e., a manuscript i the author's own handwriting (and even here an occasiona slip of the pen is not impossible). Bible translators hav usually adopted some particular edition; Luther used Eras mus's text (together with the Vulgate)—and Erasmu used his own, in making a Latin translation of the Ne Testament; Theodore de Bèze used Codex Bezae (his ow discovery); the King James' revisers the *textus receptus* o Stephanus (Paris 1553); the Revisers of 1870-81 the tex of Westcott and Hort, or one very closely resembling it; D Moffatt used Hermann Von Soden's newly published edi tion (1913). The RSV Committee had the advantage o three excellent modern editions: (*a*) Rudolf Kittel's *Biblia Hebraica*, the third edition of which was revised by Paul Kahle (1937), with further readings derived from the Dead Sea Scrolls (Isaiah and Habakkuk); (*b*) the new edition of the Septuagint by Alfred Rahlfs (1935), in addition to the great Cambridge and Göttingen editions, not yet complete, and editions, new and old, of other ancient versions; and (*c*) the 16th edition of Nestle's Greek New Testament in 1936, the 17th in 1941, together with other modern editions, including the Roman Catholic editions by A. Merk (1933), C. J. Vogels (1920), and J. M. Bover (1943). In all cases, the marginal readings in these modern editions, i.e., those found in the textual apparatus, were carefully weighed, and also many readings found in versions, ancient and modern, and in quotations made by the church fathers and other ancient writers, not given in the manual editions.

The great interpolations were first set aside, and either placed in the lower margin or omitted altogether. (1) Thus Mark 16:9-20 was retained and printed in the margin with a note, "Other texts and versions add as 16:9-20 the following passage." This "Longer Ending" probably comes from the second century, and was compiled from the other gospels, and even from the Book of Acts, as a list of the appearances of the Risen Lord. It may even be a fragment from some early Easter sermon! An ancient Armenian manuscript attributes it to "the presbyter Ariston." Certainly it was not written by Mark: the style and vocabulary are not his. The purpose of the addition, in most ancient manuscripts, was doubtless to complete the Gospel of Mark. The final sentence, "For they were afraid," seemed an unsatisfactory conclusion; many scholars, even today, hold that the Gospel of

Mark must once have continued past this point, the original conclusion being lost at an early date, before Matthew and Luke made use of Mark in compiling their gospels. There is also a "Shorter Ending," in some manuscripts taking the place of the Longer Ending, in others combined with it: "But they reported briefly to Peter and those with him all that they had been told. [This cancels their disobedience to the divine command in v. 8.] And after this, Jesus himself sent out by means of them, from east to west, the sacred and imperishable proclamation of eternal salvation" (RSV translation). This conclusion is not in Mark's style either; but it also rounds off the gospel, as the "Longer Ending" did, and likewise shows the influence of the other gospels (see Matt 28:16-20; Luke 24:44-49; Acts 1:1-8).

(2) Another interpolation is found in John 7:53-8:11, the story of Jesus and the adulteress, a bit of "floating tradition" which was incorporated in various manuscripts but at different places—as here or after 7:36 or after 21:24 or after Luke 21:38, or even at the end of the gospels, as if no certain place could be found for it. Later commentators tried to find a better location than any manuscript gave it; some favored Mark 12:17. But again, the style and vocabulary are against its location in any of our existing gospels. And in spite of its popularity, it is a question if the story, at least in its present form, can be authentic. Jesus apparently pronounces forgiveness without any evidence of repentance. St. Augustine, we recall, refused to let it be read at church services in the Diocese of Hippo, lest a false inference of "easy forgiveness" might be drawn by the hearers.

(3) Another and very famous interpolation is the one between 1 John 5:7 and 8, probably a fourth-century insertion

into the text in the interest of the doctrine of the Trinity. The Spanish writer Priscillian (circa A.D. 380) was the first to quote it. The earlier manuscripts, and the majority of the church fathers—all Eastern fathers, and, in the West, the great ones, Irenaeus, Tertullian, Cyprian, Jerome, Augustine—ignore the reading. It was a great improvement when the Revised Version of 1881 omitted it from the Authorized Version of 1611; in the RSV it is not mentioned.

(4) Another is the "longer reading" in Luke 22:19-20, where many manuscripts add the words (undoubtedly inspired by 1 Cor. 11:23-25), " 'Which is given for you. Do this in remembrance of me.' And likewise the cup after supper, saying, 'This cup which is poured out for you is the new covenant in my blood.' " The addition is omitted in the so-called "Western" type of text, and is one of a number of so-called "Western non-interpolations," found chiefly at the end of the Gospel of Luke (see p. 36). Fenton J. A. Hort gave them this name, and pointed out their importance. Since the "Western" text often amplifies, especially in Luke and Acts, it is extremely significant when it does not do so, i.e., when it does not interpolate. Therefore, it may very easily be true that the shorter text, preserved in the "Western" manuscripts, versions, and fathers is the true, i.e., the original, text. Further, the insertion of this passage, designed to relate the events of the Last Supper in proper sequence (bread first, wine following), only complicates the narrative, and results in the order: cup, bread, cup. Still further, the idea of a "new" covenant is Pauline, not Synoptic; it represents Paul's interpretation—or one current in the early Gentile churches—of the prophecy in Jeremiah 31:31-34. But Jeremiah's prophecy looked for-

ward to the *end* of sacrificial worship and the inauguration of a new covenant when God would put his law "within" his people and "write it upon their hearts." The result would be perfect obedience, and there would be no need of any sacrifice for sin—as the author of the Epistle to Hebrews recognized (10:18).

(5) One more example may be cited: the "ascription" at the end of the Lord's Prayer (Matt. 6:13), "For thine is the kingdom and the power and the glory, for ever. Amen." This is a very early liturgical addition to the Prayer, perhaps as early as the second century, soon after the Gospel of Matthew came into use in the Syrian or Palestinian churches. It is found in the *Didache* or *Teaching of the Twelve Apostles*, an early summary of Christian doctrine, morals, and directions for the administration of the sacraments of baptism and the Eucharist. And it is quite probably based on the great prayer of King David at the coronation of his son Solomon (see 1 Chron. 29:11-13). There is no reason to think that our Lord could not have used it, or that the earliest apostolic church did not; such ascriptions are characteristic of ancient Jewish prayer. Nor is there any reason to think that Christians ought not to use it now, in either public or private worship. It is a noble conclusion to the model prayer, and has been sanctified by many centuries of devout use. But it probably was not in the original text of the Gospel of Matthew.

There are other interpolations in Holy Scripture, in the Old Testament as well as in the New—but far fewer in the Old Testament since its text became stabilized before most of the surviving manuscripts were copied. And none of these interpolations is of anything like the length or importance of those in the New Testament. Most of them are found in the Septuagint or Greek translation—for example, the additions to Esther (see the RSV Apocrypha, pp. 82-86, where they are inserted in proper order). These additions to Esther were made, presumably, in order to correct the impression left by the "Purim scroll" in the Hebrew Bible; for, strange to tell, it never once uses the word "God."

In addition to these longer insertions into the sacred text, which were made in the days before the view came to prevail that Holy Scripture was verbally inspired and therefore could not be supplemented, there are hundreds of slight variations between manuscripts. These were the result partly of copyists' mistakes, partly of attempts to correct the mistakes, and partly of "conflations" or combinations of the errors and the corrections. Some were dictated by reverence —a motive already at work in the later evangelists' reproduction of the text of St. Mark. Matthew, for example, tones down expressions which imply too human a character in our Lord or limit his supernatural knowledge or miraculous power; Luke "spares the Twelve," and refuses to admit that the holy apostles, now saints and martyrs, were ever stupid or undiscerning or disloyal. Luke simply cannot bring himself to say of the disciples at Gethsemane, "They all forsook him and fled" (Mark 14:50).

But the impression which formerly prevailed in some quarters, that a really thorough and honest revision of the Greek text of the New Testament, or a translation based upon such a revision, would spell the end of orthodox Christianity, has been proved to be utterly mistaken.[1] Many of the most

---

[1] In 1641, Sir Symonds d'Ewes argued in Parliament, from a manuscript in the King's library, that St. Paul had addressed neither Titus nor Timothy as "bishop," the word being "an impertinent interpolation from a later date." See C. Wedgewood, *The King's Peace,* p. 439.

penetrating, and some even of the most radical, of textual critics are strongly orthodox in their theology. But they clearly recognize that there are no short cuts in textual criticism or in translation: an appeal to the later orthodox view as a solution of a textual or exegetical problem is out of the question. Textual criticism is both a science and an art; but it is first of all a science. At the same time, the uncertainty of the text is just enough to do away with the old-fashioned idea of "verbal" inspiration and an infallible "letter" of Scripture. If, say, five or ten per cent of the language of the Bible may be slightly different from its original, though not sufficient to bring any Christian doctrine into question, it is enough to destroy a bibliolatrous literalism. Uncertainty, even of a tenth of one per cent, must mean the end of infallibility. But the writers of the sacred books, and the early copyists, and some even of the early expositors, took no such view of Holy Scripture. It was all "inspired by God" (2 Tim. 3:16), yet it might be interpreted in various ways. This treasure we have "in earthen vessels" (2 Cor. 4:7)—like the books found in jars at Nag-Hammadi and Qumrân! They are most precious, and filled with light and power, even today. But they are not tape- or disc-recorded copies of oracles sent down from heaven. "Holy men of old" spoke as they were moved by the Holy Spirit (2 Peter 1:21). The Bible is an inspired literature, but it is at the same time completely human. As an ancient Jewish teacher insisted—Rabbi Ishmael in the early second century—"The Torah speaks the language of men."

A glance at the problems faced by classical scholars will make clear the advantage enjoyed by biblical editors and translators. For example, there are only *two* manuscripts of the Latin poet Lucretius, both at Leyden, one from the ninth century, the other from the tenth. In addition there are a few copies made from the codex once belonging to Giov. Francesco Poggio of Florence (1380-1459), but now lost, and a few fragments. The lost archetype to which all went back was written in uncials, i.e., in capital letters, in the fourth or fifth century, in continuous lines; the words were not separated, though the sentences were. Scholars have reconstructed the archetype: it had 302 pages each containing 26 lines, the first and last being blank. Between the ninth and tenth century, four pages disappeared from the archetype, and were copied together at the end.[2] But, worse than that, there are long lacunae where several lines have been lost (e.g., Book I, between lines 599-600, 1094-1101). These have been hypothetically restored by modern editors, most successfully by H. A. J. Munro (1864 and following), who spent his life in studying Lucretius and came to possess an uncanny felicity in expressing the ancient poet's own thoughts in his characteristic vocabulary and metre. One has only to examine the context, parallel passages, and the Lucretian language and technical terminology as a whole to realize how apt and probable these restorations are. Not all scholars accept them, but the majority do. But by contrast there is nothing like this in the biblical text, either in the Old Testament or the New. There are textual variants, i.e., slightly different readings, but no obvious lacunae, with lines left unfinished or beginning without a noun or subject or main verb. Some passages in the Apocrypha, it is true, do

[2] See W. H. D. Rouse's edition in the Loeb Classical Library, 1924, p. xvii.

fall into this category, and here the versions help us. For example, a whole long passage is now restored in the RSV translation of Sirach 26:19-27, though it is placed in the margin, where also will be found other variant readings and additions, many of them from the recently recovered Hebrew text of the work. In 2 Esdras 7, Robert L. Bensly's fragment of the Old Latin version (discovered and published in 1875) has supplied a long passage, vv. 36-105, now found in the RV and RSV—a section of great importance for the course of the argument.

It is true, there are places in both Old and New Testament, as well as in the Apocrypha, where scholars have suspected omissions, but no one has had the hardihood to prepare a hypothetical restoration of what the ancient manuscripts omitted. For one thing, the biblical manuscripts are far more numerous, both in the original language and in the versions, while the quotations in the writings of the church fathers, the rabbis, and others are vastly more numerous than is the case with classical works; and for another, the text of both Testaments has been held to be sacred, and hence was most carefully safeguarded, for so long a time that fewer errors and far fewer omissions have been found. Here again, the contrast with classical works is most marked. For example, in the Oxford edition of Plato, Professor John Burnet restored 10 lines to the dialogue known as the First Alcibiades (133c, lines 8-17) from a quotation made by the church father Eusebius in his *Praeparatio Evangelica* (XI. 27.3=551a). We now recognize how important and really crucial to the argument these lines are: man acquires self-knowledge by knowing God. This is a reply to the popular maxim of the Sophists, "Man is the measure of all things." Not so, says Plato, not man but God is the measure—or as a Hebrew or a Christian would say, "God is our judge. 'The fear of the Lord is the beginning of wisdom.' " As Plato said, "It is by looking to God that we use the best mirror of the human soul and its virtue." (Compare Paul's idea in 1 Cor. 13:12, 2 Cor. 3:7—4:6.) And all this leads up to the famous statement, which some take to be the first intimation in the West of a principle which was eventually destined to lead to Gnosticism: "Self-knowledge, we agree, is wisdom."

Accidental omissions, especially when lines began or ended with similar-looking or similar-sounding words or phrases, are common in all ancient manuscripts (similar-sounding, because copyists often wrote from dictation, one person reading aloud, slowly, while a room full of scribes wrote out the copies). But these omissions are easily controlled and corrected from other manuscripts, versions, and quotations by church fathers and other ancient writers. Occasionally an error will get perpetuated in all—or almost all—manuscripts, and only a genius will hit upon the right conjecture for its correction. Thus John 19:29 reads, "So they put a sponge full of the vinegar on hyssop and held it to his mouth." This sounded clear enough—and biblical enough— to the vast majority of scribes, and so got handed on through the centuries. But the true reading must surely have been not *hyssōpō* (hyssop) but *hyssō*, a javelin or short spear—every Roman soldier was armed with two javelins and a short two-edged sword. The conjecture was first made by Joachim Camerarius of Tübingen (1500-74), and now we find it supported by an eleventh-century minuscule manuscript, 476*, at present in London. There is no reason in the nature of things, or in the nature of paleography, why a very late manuscript should not contain a good reading which has survived from the very first copying of the New Testament books.[3]

I wish a similar solution were possible in another case. In his great essay on Isis and Osiris, which I translated in my *Hellenistic Religions* (1953), Plutarch says—or his manuscripts say—that the chest which floated along the coast from the Nile Delta to Byblos in Syria finally drifted ashore and was caught in a clump of "heather" (*ereikē*) which was later used—as a tree—to give support to the house built around it. Now let no one underrate heather, which stands for many things, loyalty, patriotism, fellowship, and other virtues, certainly among the Scots. But does it grow in Syria? Yes, it does! It is even said to grow into a bush, sometimes the shape and size of a tree! But the story sounds strange, as from some "faery land afar" where magic is an everyday occurrence, and a tuft of heather can provide safe anchorage for a sea-going chest, freighted with the body of a god. If Plutarch had written in English rather than Greek, and if one of his manuscripts now seemed blurred at this point, some critics would surely suspect that "heather" was obviously a mistake for "feather"—and a "feather tree" would mean a feather *palm*. Indeed, some scholars (without

[3] In the thirteenth-century chancel of St. Mary's Church, Pulborough, in Sussex, the dossal behind the high altar shows a Latin cross in red with two javelins standing transversely behind it, like a St. Andrew's cross. On the tip of one of the javelins is a sponge. This is a very different conception from that of the "hyssop rod" and spear (as in the Saxon crucifix in Romsey Abbey). The rod is a long thin pole, neither a "hyssop" nor a weapon—nor is it the "reed" named by Mark and Matthew but omitted by Luke.

resorting to English) hold that the tree *was* a palm.[4] But the dictionary is no help at this point. The conjecture must stand alone, or fall, if unconvincing.

Again, there are words which occur only once (*hapax legomena*) and are unknown elsewhere than in this one instance of use in the Bible—or in other ancient writings. The "sacred stone that fell from the sky" and was carefully preserved in Ephesus (Acts 19:35) is a very probable rendering of the word *diopetēs* or *diospetēs*, but we find it nowhere else. Some take it to mean a very old wooden statue of the goddess which (according to legend) had fallen from heaven; but we cannot say whether it was a statue or not. Some very ancient "statues" bore only a slight resemblance to the human form; most of the earliest Greek statues were of wood, not stone; the sacred stone of Cybele, taken from nearby Pessinus to Rome after the battle of Cannae, was probably a black meteorite, treasured from earlier ages of animism. This is all we can say; the rest is conjecture, though a very probable one.

The importance of textual study, that is of manuscripts and ancient versions, is clearly evident from the marginal readings of the Revised Standard Version. In Genesis 4:8, Cain says to his brother Abel, "Let us go out to the field"— according to the Samaritan text, the Greek and the Syriac translations (see also the Vulgate). But the Hebrew lacks the words of Cain's invitation to his brother, and leaves a

---

[4] William Baxter in the translation of Plutarch's *Morals* "by several hands," published in 1691, called it "a certain Thicket of Heath (or *Tamarisk*)"—which had hastily grown into a tree. (Isis and Osiris, ch. xv, 357a.)

meaningless lacuna which the AV patched up by reading "Cain talked with Abel." In 4:15 the Greek, Syriac, and Vulgate have "Not so!" where the Hebrew has the far less probable "Therefore"—a word which completely ignores both the logic and the dramatic sequence of the narrative. In 10:5 the RSV supplies the indispensable words, "These are the sons of Japheth," from the parallels in vv. 20 and 31. Without this sentence the conclusion of the paragraph is garbled. In 19:17 the Greek, Syriac, and Latin Vulgate have "they" instead of "he" (as read in the Hebrew); this is obviously the correct reading, which the Hebrew has somehow lost. Another strange omission is in 21:9, where the Greek and Latin have "with her son Isaac," words which are obviously required by the sense. In v. 16 it is the child Ishmael who wept, not the mother Hagar—as v. 17 shows. But this reading is that of the Greek, not the Hebrew. The Hebrew of Gen. 24:67 has the meaningless "Sarah his mother"—as if the mother-in-law accompanied the bride to her chamber, surely a most extraordinary way in which to begin a happy married life! But the versions omit the phrase. In 32:49 the "pillar" is found only in the Samaritan text, not in the Hebrew; but the meaning clearly requires it. In 36:2 "son" is surely right, as in the Samaritan, the Greek, and the Syriac—not "daughter" as in the Hebrew. The same is true of v. 14. A similar phenomenon is found in 38:5 where the Greek reads "she" instead of "he." Another example of wrong number is found in the Hebrew of 41:8, where the Greek reads "it," not "them." In 41:48 the meaningless "which were" becomes clear in the Samaritan and the Greek, "the seven years when there was plenty in the land of Egypt." So in v. 56: it is the storehouses that were opened in the years of famine (Greek and Vulgate; cf. Syriac), not "all that was in them." In this instance the AV was correct: "Joseph opened all the storehouses." A very striking omission occurs in the Hebrew of 44:4. "Why have you stolen my silver cup?" is restored from the Greek and the Vulgate. Without it the continuation in v. 5 is impossible: "Is it not from this that my lord drinks, and by this that he divines?" The order, "Command them," in 45:19, is clearly correct (see Greek and Latin), not the Hebrew "You are commanded." The social condition of the people of Egypt, and the contrast between their status and that of the priests, is ignored in the present text of 47:21, "He [Pharaoh or Joseph] removed them to the cities"; but it is preserved in the Samaritan, Greek, and Vulgate: "He made slaves of them from one end of Egypt to the other." This condition characterized the Egyptian populace for centuries, and has in fact continued until recently. In 49:4 "he" should surely be "you," as in the Greek, the Syriac, and the Targum. The meaningless "Shiloh" (*sh-y-l-h*) correctly becomes "he . . . to whom it belongs," in 49:10, on the basis of the Syriac and the Targums. Though a favorite of mystical interpreters, for many centuries, and the name of a battlefield in the American Civil War, the meaning clearly requires the abandonment of "Shiloh" as a proper noun or a title. The obscure line in the Blessing of Jacob (49:26b), in the Hebrew, becomes clear, beautiful, and moving in the RSV, based on the Greek version:

The blessings of your father
    are mighty beyond the blessings of the eternal mountains,
    the bounties of the everlasting hills.

These examples are all taken from the Book of Genesis. Equally striking, equally important renderings are to be found throughout the Old Testament and the New, and also the RSV Apocrypha, based upon the comparison of ancient manuscripts, texts, and versions—including the quotations found in the ancient Jewish writings and in the church fathers. These are the result of more than three centuries of careful, patient textual study of the Bible, and they must be taken into account by all serious students of Holy Scripture. If we follow the example of the King James revisers, we shall certainly welcome them, rather than try to maintain the superiority of a translation which, although it was the best in its time, was based upon far fewer manuscripts and editions, and could not possibly have referred to readings which were unknown in 1611.

2. Principles of Translation

There are certain general principles which apply to all translations of ancient books into modern languages, especially the English rendering of the classics. Some of these principles are particularly relevant to the translation of the Bible, from ancient Hebrew and Greek into modern English; and some of them are relevant only under modification, in view of the special subject matter, style, or linguistic structure of the Bible in its original tongues. We may see all this more clearly, perhaps, if we study a statement of principles made by a learned translator of a century ago. In the Preface to the second edition (1875) of his famous translation of the Dialogues of Plato, Benjamin Jowett set forth the principles which had guided him in his *magnum opus*, which had first appeared only four years before. It was a time when principles of translation were being widely discussed. Matthew Arnold, the leading literary man of the day, had written a long essay "On Translating Homer" (1861). Alexander Fraser Tytler's *Principles of Translation* (1791) was still the standard of judgment in literary circles. And it was well known that at Westminster Abbey two groups of scholars were at work revising once more the authorized English translation of the Bible.

Dr. Jowett felt himself obliged to set forth the problems he had faced in translating Plato, and the principles upon which he had solved them. His task had proved far greater than he had anticipated—the translation had taken five years and filled four thick octavo volumes. Though he referred to it as "only a translation" (*Letters*, 1897, p. 182), the work was really a superb interpretation of Plato, the Plato of traditional Christian philosophy and theology, from Clement of Alexandria to Dean Inge and Archbishop Temple. There have been other translations—the Bohn Library translation, for example, which I began purchasing in 1905, and almost despaired of ever understanding. (The famous Philadelphia bookseller, William H. Allen, on Walnut Street, once described it in a catalogue as "a fairly intelligible translation, provided you use the Greek as a pony!") There have been other translators, some of them very critical of Jowett, with his "golden haze of scriptural language" and his neglect of the contemporary fourth-century issues

· *131*

which confronted the philosophers. But read the Greek! *It* has a "golden haze," the most perfect, urbane, intellectual Attic ever written. And the "scriptural" overtones are appropriate in an English version: they match the epic, lyric, and tragic overtones in Plato's own style and composition. Plato's style has the "mellow glory" of an autumn harvest at the end of two centuries of Greek philosophy—we often forget that it began long before Socrates and the Sophists. In the remarkable new revised edition of Jowett's *Plato* (Oxford 1953), the editors have rightly refused to rewrite the work, though basing it now on Burnet's edition of the Greek text (Oxford 1900-07) instead of the nineteenth-century text of Stallbaum, and deftly substituting better wording wherever it was demanded by present-day scholarship.

This new edition (by D. J. Allan and H. H. Dale[5] of Balliol College, where Jowett had been Master) is itself an example of a judicious and very successful "revised version" of a classic English translation, and rewards careful study by all who are interested in the problems and principles of the art.

Jowett fully recognized that "the interests of the Greek and the English are often at war with one another," and one has to choose between giving the precise, literal meaning and emphasis of the Greek or an English rendering which is not only accurate but readable, that is, in good literary style, in English as beautiful as Plato's Greek. Both are works of art, the Greek original and the English translation —as was also the King James Version of 1611, which as

[5] The former is now Professor of Greek at Glasgow.

Mr. Dale died July 30, 1954.

some have said is "far more literary" than the original Hebrew or Greek Scriptures. Jowett erred, if at all, by too great attention to the English, and his revisers have endeavored to bring the version closer to the Greek text—much as the English revisers of the Bible in 1870-85 and the Revised Standard Version Committee in 1938-57 did in bringing the biblical text into closer relation to the Hebrew Old Testament and the Greek New Testament and Apocrypha. But, again, this was a task of revision, not of rewriting. The great translators, who put themselves fully into their work, usually do this. Gilbert Murray's Euripides, for example, has been accused of being "more Murray than Euripides"; but look at the Greek—again and again what seems at first too modern and too English to be Euripidean turns out to have a perfect justification in the text of the original, granted the right of a translator to choose one interpretation and give that, rather than aim at several and fall flat. Take the final choruses of Euripides, for example; they sound, in translation, too full of the ethos of the early 1900's. But on consulting the original the translation appears to be fully justified; evidently "our Euripides the human" was also Euripides the modern!—one more tie between our century and the fifth century B.C. in Athens, with its wars, its skepticism, its disillusion, its religious doubts and unrest, its social uncertainty and longing for security, its limited satisfaction with very small crumbs of spiritual and ethical assurance.

If a translation is to be any good, it must be addressed to the times in which it is written. One reason why the Revised Version of 1881-85 failed, and along with it the American Standard Edition of the Revised Version in 1901, was that it did not address the world in which men lived. There were passages in both editions, the English and the American, even more archaic than the basic text, the version of 1611— the principles adopted by the revisers required the choice of Elizabethan or Jacobean words "still in common use," as substitutes for those which had gone out of use or had changed in meaning. Such archaism was foredoomed to failure—like that of some of the ponderous translations of Greek and Latin classics likewise produced in the nineteenth century, which endeavored to convey a sense of antiquity by using -eth and -est in the speeches by Homer's heroes! But the King James translators of the Bible, like Tyndale and Coverdale and the Bishops before them, used -eth and -est because it was the speech of everyday. There was nothing archaic or "biblical" about such forms. They were not artificially "archaizing," like furniture dealers who "antique" good tables and chairs with make-believe worm-holes.

Jowett, who wrote magisterial Victorian prose with the ease of a journalist writing a news story, insisted, first of all, that an English translation "ought to be idiomatic and interesting, not only to the scholar, but to the unlearned reader." And surely this is one characteristic of the "Authorized Version" of the Bible. On page after page of the Bodleian copy of the Bishops' Bible in which their changes were registered, usually in the margin, the improvements in accuracy and idiom made by the King James men are clearly evident. For example, Luke 1:17 "perfect people" was crossed out, and in its place was inserted "people prepared" (still the rendering of the RSV). On the other hand in v. 19 "was sent" became "am sent"—good sixteenth-century style: *vide* Shakespeare!—but not quite the modern idiom; the

RSV has gone back to the Bishops' rendering: "I was sent to speak to you," surely a better locution, more natural with its finite verb in the past tense than with a present passive (now rarely used). Or in v. 20, "not be able to speak" became in 1611 "not able"; today we say "and unable" (so the RSV). These are small matters, but as Jowett held, and as all good translators recognize, small details of idiom (or its absence!) make or break a translation.

> The little more, and how much it is!
> The little less, and what worlds away!

It is still "the little foxes that spoil the vineyards" (Song 2:15).

There is, of course, no such thing as translating word-for-word, as if each Greek or Hebrew word had an exact equivalent in English—or any other language. Any examiner who has read students' language papers is perfectly familiar with this: the tragic failures result from a kind of linguistic game of checkers, where every black piece has a white equivalent, and the dictionary words, when substituted for the original, simply make no sense. For example, "And it became in one of the days teaching of him the people in the temple and evangelizing they stood up the high priests and the scribes with the presbyters and they said saying against him, They tell us in such authority these things you do . . ." (Luke 20:1-2). Any passage will illustrate the possibility of this game of literary checkers—or dominos. But it is not translation. It is to be feared that some of the "more literal" translations of today (and yesterday!) move in this direction. What should be aimed at is not a series of "exact equivalents," designed to save the lazy student the labor entailed in a mastery of the language, but "an impression similar or nearly similar to that produced by the original." What Jowett said of translating Plato is equally true of translating the Bible.

[The translator] must carry in his mind a comprehensive view of the whole work, of what has preceded and what is to follow—as well as of the meaning of particular passages. His version should be based, in the first instance, on an intimate knowledge of the text; but the precise order and arrangement of the words may be left to fade out of sight, when the translation begins to take shape. He must form a general idea of the two languages, and reduce the one to the terms of the other. His work should be rhythmical and varied; the right admixture of words and syllables, and even of letters, should be attended to; above all, it should be equable in style. There must also be quantity which is necessary in prose as well as in verse: clauses, sentences, paragraphs, must be in due proportion. Metre and even rhyme may be rarely admitted; though neither is a legitimate element of prose writing, they may help to lighten a cumbrous expression (cp. *Symposium* 185d, 197, 198). The translation should retain as far as possible the characteristic qualities of the ancient writer—his freedom, grace, simplicity, stateliness, weight, precision; or the best part of him will be lost to the English reader. It should be read as an original work, and should also be the most faithful transcript which can be made of the language from which the translation is taken, consistently with the first requirement of all, that it be English. Further, the translation being English, it should also be perfectly intelligible in itself without reference to the Greek, the English being really the more lucid and exact of the two languages.

This great Preface raises points that will occur to everyone familiar with the translation of the Bible. A sense of the
whole; familiarity with the rest of a writer's work, e.g., St.
Paul's; a feeling for the use made of the Old Testament in
the New and for the attitude held toward ancient Scripture
by later writers; a readiness to sacrifice needless peculiarities
in Hebrew and Greek idiom, e.g., the constant parataxis,
"*and . . . and . . . and*"; the use of rhythm and on
occasion metre, to be found even in the RSV, e.g., Matt. 7:2,
"The measure you give will be the measure you get," or
Luke 1:33, "Of his kingdom there will be no end," or Isa.
11:9,

> For the earth shall be full of the knowledge of the Lord
>   As the waters cover the sea.

No one will question that these words are English, perfectly intelligible, thoroughly idiomatic, and magnificent as
translations. *Pace* Mr. Somerset Maugham and others who
dislike "cloudy" metaphors and similes, the waters *do* "cover
the sea." For the ancients, especially the Hebrews, the sea
included both top and bottom, and "the great deep" was
the awesome term for it. God—or a spirit—could "walk" in
the "deep places" of it; monsters swam in its depths—

> There is that Leviathan,
> Whom thou hast made to take his
>   pastime therein (Psalm 104:26 BCP).

They lacked the Roman navigator's easy parlance, which
spoke of the ocean "floor" but meant the surface (*aequor*);
or the Greek's concern only for swift voyages, unhindered
by adverse winds, and profitable trading en route; for the

Hebrews dreaded the sea, and were never at home on it, or in it. This provides part of the terrible background in the allegorical tale of Jonah: the Jews' horror of deep water, horror still vividly real in the stories of refugee ships on their way to Israel soon after the last World War.—This slight digression may be justified, as it illustrates the kind of feeling as well as thought a translator must possess when he undertakes to render Greek and Hebrew idiom into something approaching it, not in literal word-equivalents, but in parallel English idiom, with similar overtones of feeling as well as connotations of ideas.

When Jowett insisted upon "the most faithful transcript which can be made," he was surely not thinking of such a principle as Bishop Lightfoot proposed and constantly advocated in the 1870-81 revision, viz., "the principle of faithfulness," by which he meant the use of identically the same English words to represent the same Greek words, and "as far as possible" in the same order. Theoretically, Lightfoot's translation could have fallen back into Greek with the greatest ease, like a casting into its mould; theoretically, no schoolboy could have asked for a more reliable "pony"— as many a divinity student has discovered! This was not the King James principle, which called for variety and recognized the principle of writing good English (as Jowett also insisted), not "translation English." It was this ideal of "faithfulness" that rendered the greatest disservice to the Revised Version, making it too literal to be accurate, or readable, or interesting. The latest revision, in the long line that began with Tyndale, has observed the King James principle, and has allowed for variation in rendering, choice of idiom, and feeling for words in their present meaning and connotation, especially in particular contexts and sequences of thought.

Jowett goes on to discuss the contrasts between Greek and English. Similar contrasts and still others exist between Hebrew and English:

(1) "The structure of the Greek language is partly adversative and alternative, and partly inferential"—a feature which is less common in modern languages: "we cannot have two *buts* or two *fors* in the same sentence, and our negatives are much simplified."

(2) "The formation of the sentence and of the paragraph greatly differs in Greek and English"—Plato's sentences sometimes run into one another, and "paragraphs are few and far between." It is at least one likeness of St. Paul to Plato that the same is often true of his sentences!

(3) Even greater difficulty arises from "the restriction of the use of genders"—which scarcely exists in modern English, though there are some persons who insist upon referring to the church and the nation as "she." The same personification is occasionally found in the Bible: Israel is a bride, a widow, an abandoned wife; the church is a bride, a temple, even, perhaps, "the woman clothed with the sun" (Rev. 12:1-6); but these metaphors are open and obvious, and the requisite pronoun is specified in advance, not drawn from common usage (as *ecclesia* is "she," because a feminine noun).

(4) Still another characteristic of Greek which cannot be imitated in English is the relation of various parts of sentences, which can become extremely involved and trip up all but the most careful and wary. "The Greek appears to have

had an ear or intelligence for a long and complicated sentence which is rarely to be found in modern nations; and in order to bring the Greek down to the level of the modern, we must break up the long sentence into two or more short ones." Again St. Paul comes to mind, and the Epistle to Hebrews, and some parts of the Apocrypha; though as a rule the Old Testament was free from this difficulty.

(5) The repetition of words rarely troubled the Greek; it usually annoys or even irritates us. The literal translation of Greek often results in a tautology which a modern writer would avoid—unless he is a lawyer or a scientist, for whom precision matters more than everything, as it evidently did for the ancient Greek!

(6) Hence, Jowett concludes, "the excellence of a translation will consist, not merely in the faithful rendering of words, or in the composition of a sentence only, or yet of a single paragraph, but in the colour and style of the whole work. Equability of tone is best attained by the exclusive use of familiar and idiomatic words. . . . No word, however expressive and exact, should be employed, which makes the reader stop and think, or unduly attracts attention by difficulty or peculiarity, or disturbs the effect of the surrounding language. In general the style of one author is not appropriate to another." Archaic expressions are therefore to be avoided; and metaphors, which ordinarily do not transfer easily from one language to another, should be represented by substitutes.

Finally, (7) "it is a mistaken attempt at precision always to translate the same Greek word by the same English word. There is no reason why in the New Testament *dikaiosunē* should always be rendered 'righteousness,' or *diathēkē* 'covenant.' "—Could Jowett have heard of the Revisers' "principle of faithfulness"? If so, it is a pity they did not hear or heed this protest from the greatest translator of his time!

Jowett's Preface is a classic, and deserves careful study by all persons interested in, or concerned with, the translation of either Holy Scripture or the classics into modern English. The brief summary here presented, and the few suggestions offered for the application of his principles, *mutatis mutandis*, to the translation of the Bible, are only a slight indication of what is still to be learned from one who was not only a master of Greek but of English, "pure and undefiled."

3. *Special Problems*

A problem of special seriousness in translating the Bible, but not confronted by translators of prose, like Jowett, is the rendering of ancient poetry in modern prose or verse. Hebrew poetry was not metrical, like Greek and Latin, nor rhythmic, like some modern. Instead, it was parallelistic (see p. 86), usually with lines approximately equal in length, measured by stresses (usually three), and in which the parallelism was either repetitive, adversative, or progressive, the last sometimes being in step-form. For example, *repetitive*:

> Summon thy might, O God;
>   show thy strength, O God, thou
>   who hast wrought for us. (Psalm 68:28)

Or *adversative:*

> O God, thou knowest my folly;
>> the wrongs I have done are not
>>> hidden from thee. (Psalm 69:5)

Or *progressive,* by steps:

> Draw near to me, redeem me,
>> set me free because of my enemies! (Psalm 69:18)

There are also other forms of Hebrew poetry, and of Hebrew parallelism: for example, the chiastic form where the first and last lines are parallel, the second and the next to last, and so on. A good example is found in the saying of Jesus in Matt. 7:6, which was probably spoken in Aramaic (the poetry of which is closely allied in form to the Hebrew):

> Do not give dogs what is holy;
>> and do not throw your pearls before swine,
>> lest they trample them underfoot
> and turn to attack you.

Here lines 2 and 3 refer to swine, lines 1 and 4 to dogs. Chiasmus (from "crossing," the letter *chi* in Greek resembling a St. Andrew's cross) may become far more elaborate, as lines in a verse or stanza increase in number. Instead of four lines there may be as many as eight or ten, ascending and descending like a step ladder: lines 1-2-3-4-5 being balanced by lines 10-9-8-7-6. Professor Nils Lund, in his book *Chiasmus in the New Testament* (1942), has traced many examples from both Old Testament and New.

The actual translation of the Hebrew is simple enough, but the problem of making the English sufficiently rhythmic, not only readable but also (for some purposes and in some churches) singable, i.e., the Psalms and the New Testament Canticles and some of the poetry in the Apocrypha—this is a very real problem.

It is further complicated by the fact that much of the biblical poetry is very familiar to Bible-readers and church-goers, especially the Psalms and Canticles, and certain chapters in the prophets. Forty per cent of the Old Testament is poetry, and far more of the New than many translations indicate. For some readers or hearers, as we have seen, this long familiarity with the traditional text makes it almost impossible to change. Take the 23rd Psalm, for example. The RSV translation is still almost identical with the King James Version—except for the archaic personal endings of the verbs, -eth and -est. The RSV is closer to the Hebrew: "I fear no evil" rather than "I will fear no evil." And it is more modern: "my cup overflows" for "runneth over"; "shall dwell" for "will dwell." But fortunately the King James Version was extraordinarily accurate at this point, and clearly superior to Coverdale, whose version the Prayer Book still retains. The same is true of the Lord's Prayer and the Ten Commandments, which it would be difficult to change, but fortunately need not be altered very much. What is especially needful, in parts of the Bible as universally familiar as these, is more instruction by pastors and teachers, so that the full meaning of the language will be understood. For example, "You shall not kill," RSV (or "Thou shalt not kill," King James Version) really means "Thou shalt do no murder," as in the Prayer Book Version. It is not a Buddhist rule forbidding any extermination of animals, or an ancient dictum of "reverence for life," but a commandment forbidding homicide. And it requires the deepening of motive and widening of application found in Matt. 5:21-26.

But there are passages which are so familiar that people no longer listen—as there are songs (and hymns!) where the familiar tune lulls us to inattention; we could almost sing (or hear sung) nonsense-words if the music remained the same! And there are passages in the Bible so familiar that we *think* we know what the cherished biblical phrases mean, but really do not, for we have never examined them. (The same is true of the Qumrân documents, as Professor Kurt Schubert has pointed out—we do not really understand until we read the biblical phrases in a wholly new setting, and with a new group of implications and applications.) Take the middle section of Isa. 61 and the whole of Chapter 63; the familiarity of the language and the sublimity of one or two verses close our ears to the thorough jingoism of the chapters. One of them, Isa. 63, is the passage appointed for the Epistle on Monday in Holy Week, for it was mystically or allegorically interpreted to refer to the Passion of Christ. But no allegorical interpretation can survive a clear, accurate translation of the Hebrew text of III Isaiah! The same is true of many of the Psalms, where "enemies" were interpreted to mean "sins" or "demons" who attacked the souls of the righteous. John Mason Neale and Richard F. Littledale's great four-volume *Commentary on the Psalms from Primitive and Mediaeval Writers* (1874) is a fascinating repository of this kind of exegesis, popular among the church fathers and in the Middle Ages; so is the commentary in Bishop Alfred Barry's *Teacher's Prayer Book* (1884). Allegorical interpretation was a necessity once, during long centuries before the modern historical view of the Bible or the general history of religion was understood, but it cannot be defended today. In the ancient world it arose, first, in the interpretation of Homer and the Greek myths; it was widely practiced by the Stoic teachers and others; it was adopted by Philo of Alexandria, the Jewish philosopher and exegete of the Bible; and from him it was taken over by the early Christian teachers and expositors, especially in Alexandria. But one whole school, that in Antioch, stood out against it as long as they could. In the West it spread far and wide in the Middle Ages, chiefly as a result of St. Augustine's teaching. With the Reformation came a reaction (see p. 54), and the plain, literal, historical sense was made really primary; the three other "senses" of Scripture (see p. 53) were recognized for what they were— pious fancies (not always pious!).

Hence a modern translator of the Bible cannot fall back upon allegorism to smooth the rough passages; and he must be true to the original text. Hence also there is today a fresh demand for historical study and interpretation, and a religious interpretation which recognizes the principle of development and growth. This is fully provided for, in the Scripture itself: "You have heard that it was said . . . but I say"; "In many and various ways God spoke of old to our fathers . . . but in these last days . . . by a Son"; "No prophecy of Scripture is of any private interpretation" (Matt. 5:21-48; Heb. 1:1-2; 2 Pet. 1:20).

The gloriously beautiful poetry of the Bible is sometimes concentrated in a single word or phrase: "the outskirts of his ways"—God is a God who "hides himself," though he is the Savior (Job 26:14; Isa. 45:15). This is real poetry. It is like the fresh, virile poetry of St. Patrick, with his perfect blend of striking figure and keen imagery with simple language; for example, the lines in his *Breastplate*,

> His bursting from the spicèd tomb,
> His riding up the heavenly way.
> (*The Hymnal, 1940*, No. 268)

It is like John Milton's "golden tressèd sun" and "hornèd moon," in his Paraphrase of Psalm 136 (*English Hymnal*, No. 532). For it has all the freshness of dawn, the beginning of a great poetic tradition in Hebrew literature. For an extended example, read the magnificent strophe in Deut. 33:13-17, which almost proves Macaulay's thesis that with poetry as with wine, the oldest is the best.

This is one reason why many have questioned the use of a word which recurs repeatedly, in the new version, and has crowded out an older and very familiar one: the RSV Psalter consistently uses "steadfast love" in place of "loving kindness." By some readers this is thought to be a great loss. But upon further reflection it may be viewed as great gain. Clustering about the traditional conception of divine benevolence are ideas really incompatible with the Christian faith and with the fullest experience of life. God is no Santa Claus, concerned only with giving, or a fabulously rich Oriental potentate who can shower his children with benefits —but who, strangely, does not do so. This conception of God forces us back to consider the problems faced by ancient religion, as by Adeimantus in Plato's *Republic* (II.365e), who held that if there are gods they take little notice of men, and by all the schools of philosophy which dealt with the problems of theism. If God is infinitely powerful and good, how can he permit the suffering of the innocent and helpless?

The affirmation of one of the psalmists,

> Once was I young, now am I old,
> Yet saw I never the righteous forsaken,
>   nor his seed begging their bread (Psalm 37:25)

—this childish pollyanna creed is contradicted on page after page of the Psalter itself, where the cries of the poor and the persecuted rise up to heaven. The Book of Job is concerned with the problem, but finds no solution beyond a silent acquiescence in the divine sovereignty, the divine inscrutability: God knows best. But the New Testament does not accept this solution as final. Christ on his cross requires an answer, and faith refuses to acquiesce in a "reverent agnosticism." It breaks through to the triumphant affirmation of Christ's victory—and ours—over sin and suffering, over pain and death, and it shouts its new credo for all the world to hear:

> O death, where is thy victory?

—"I am sure that neither death, nor life . . . will be able to separate us from the love of God in Christ Jesus our Lord" (1 Cor. 15:55; Rom. 8:38f.). God not only cares about the sufferings and frustrations of his children, but he is actually involved in them:

> In all their affliction he was afflicted,
>   and the angel of his presence saved them;
> in his love and in his pity he redeemed them;
>   he lifted them up and carried them all the
>   days of old. (Isa. 63:9)

[There is a variant reading which sounds as if it had once been a marginal comment: "*He* did not afflict."]

The modern world is aware that our life is a struggle.

The opulent Garden of Innocence was left, long ago: the story is as true economically and politically as it is psychologically, and the effort to achieve general welfare is itself half the struggle, no mere panacea for "social injustice." Two world wars, and many more, have proved that the conditions of human survival involve far more than dependence upon supernatural benevolence. An adequate conception of God requires us to believe that he shares the struggle, even sharing its defeats, and does not end it all by irresistible, omnipotent fiat. All this enables us to see into the deeper meaning of the Hebrew word which our forefathers translated by "loving kindness." Not that God's "loving kindness" is a wrong conception; it is merely inadequate. The word *chesedh* means "love, kindness, benevolence, good will, favor, benefit, mercy, grace, piety, even beauty." A Jewish saint was a *chasid*. The mercies of the Lord were his *chasadhim*. But above all the note stressed by the psalmists is loyalty, steadfastness:

> The Lord's own mercies fail not

—"for his steadfast love endures for ever"; this is the theme of Psalm 136, so beautifully paraphrased by John Milton, with the reiterated refrain,

> *For his mercies ay endure,*
> *Ever faithful, ever sure.*[6]

> To the Lord our God belong mercy and forgiveness;
> Though [KJV] we have rebelled against him,
>   neither have we obeyed the voice of the Lord our God,
>   (Daniel 9:9f.)

[6] *English Hymnal*, No. 532; *The Hymnal, 1940*, No. 308.

nevertheless, like a true lover, he refuses to be resentful, and continues to show his affection and loyalty.

> For the love of God is broader
>   Than the measure of man's mind;
> And the heart of the Eternal
>   Is most wonderfully kind.[7]

It was "while we were yet sinners" that "Christ died for us" (Rom. 5:8). Such unflagging love, "which will not let me go," which cannot be alienated or offended or turned into cold indifference or hate—this is what we find in our Master, our King, our Great Ally, and in him we can trust, for life and death, and beyond death. Like the desert *shayik* who demands utter loyalty from his fellow tribesmen, and reciprocally binds himself in utter loyalty to them, so God relates himself to his people; if they suffer, he suffers; if they triumph, he triumphs. This is the deepest message of the Psalms and of the Bible as a whole; and it is the message most needed by us, today. For the whole struggle of mankind for survival, physical, economic, political, ethical, not only involves certain ideas or ideals, but actually involves the person of our Creator himself, who is in the struggle with us. If the process fails and comes to nothing, it is as much his failure as ours. But he will not fail. And his "steadfast love," his utter loyalty and all the manifestations of his goodness that have their root in this virtue, are the guarantee that we shall not fail, in the end. Upon second thoughts, the sounder historical and philological interpretation of *chesedh* is the one richer in meaning and relevance, especially today.

---

[7] *English Hymnal,* No. 499; *The Hymnal, 1940,* No. 304.

Not all of the Bible is on this high level. There are passages that reflect antique ideas of God and of human life,
since the Bible is the record of both a revelation and a discovery, and the low level from which men set out is clearly
presupposed. I have mentioned the Book of Job. Its final
words are a fading *decrescendo* in three short measures,
after which "the rest is silence." The last verse reads, "And
Job died, an old man, and full of days" (Job 42:17). Here
the *American Translation* reads, "So Job died, an old man,
satisfied with life." This is superb—one of the finest "last
lines" in English literature. But it is not what the Hebrew
text says, and it reads into the book and its solution of the
problem of suffering far more than the author intended. It
leaves one with the impression that the valiant old ethical
warrior's unflagging faith was eventually victorious and
satisfied. But Job was no heroic figure in a Greek tragedy,
like the Oedipus of Sophocles, probing and pondering the
conflicting maze of human motives and emotions, analyzing
them, and finding at last some consolation in human love and
loyalty—

> The blind old wanderer who vainly strove
> To flee his fate and flout the will of Jove . . .
> At last he died, and sleeps beneath this hill.

Instead, Job is a religious figure, tormented by the total
failure of the traditional promise of prosperity for the
righteous, and the author recognizes the utterly inscrutable
nature of the will of God—inscrutable to us. The solution
lies on another level. Out of the furnace of affliction comes a
new and thrice refined faith: God is good, God is just, and
his love is everlasting and unfailing; we can trust his loyalty,
even if we cannot understand his ways.

150 ·

There are many more passages which might be examined, where greater accuracy in translation brings out the real meaning of the text and its greater relevance to human life today and every day, or shows more clearly the stages through which God's unfolding revelation of himself, his purposes, and his ways has gone. Such passages will be found in Job 19:26, where the ambiguous "from my flesh" is perhaps all that can be done with the obscure Hebrew *mibsari;* or Isa. 7:14, where "virgin" is found only in the Septuagint, not the Hebrew, but which marks the earliest beginning of a prophecy destined to grow in definiteness until its fulfilment came in "the Birth of the Messiah" which "took place in this way" (Matt. 1:18), i.e., as a fulfilment of the *Septuagint* interpretation of the divine oracle (see p. 23) ; or Isa. 53:11, "He shall see the *fruit* of the travail of his soul and be satisfied," where the KJV is too literal, "see *of* the travail," and where *mēamal* clearly bears a substantive meaning, something produced by, or resulting from, the travail of soul.

There have been many theological translations in the past, as well as theological commentaries and expositions—which should always follow, not precede, the translation. The translation should be as accurate as is possible, regardless of theological exegesis. Then, but only then, the theologian may begin to base his systematic structure on its foundation. Too often, "theological" commentaries and translations have strained or altered the translation in the interest of some one particular theological view or system. The process began even before translations were required (2 Pet. 3:15f.). Much has been made of Paul's "theology" in modern times. The earliest interpreters show interest, but no determination to compel Paul to "stand and deliver" a system of dogmatic theology. For example, we have been told that Paul had a clear-cut terminology based upon a clear-cut idea of the relation between body, soul, and spirit, and that he used "flesh" with one, and only one, clear-cut meaning. But this is obviously mistaken. Paul had no dictionary, and he often used synonyms, as did everyone who spoke ancient Greek. St. Irenaeus, one of his earliest interpreters, was under no such illusion. He held that the saved will rise in spirit, soul, and body, while the damned will go away in soul and body— with no mention of spirit (Irenaeus, *Against Heresies*, V. 6-12). Paul sometimes uses a similar dichotomy, as in 1 Cor. 5:5, where a grave sinner is to be cut off from the congregation and delivered to Satan "for the destruction of the flesh [through accident, disease, or otherwise], that his *spirit* may be saved in the day of the Lord Jesus." (Here Paul ignores the contention of modern theologians who insist he thinks only in terms of resurrection of the body!) True, the "flesh" is the sin-infected part of man's nature, and cannot really be salvaged; the resurrection is to be the raising-up of the transformed "body"—or rather, perhaps, of an entirely new body (1 Cor. 15:38, 49-54)—but Paul nowhere provides his readers with a glossary explaining the precise sense in which he always used his terms. And he did not, as a matter of fact, use them always in the same sense. Neither did Irenaeus: the creation of man was like a sculptor making his model of clay, i.e., by "building it up"—his *plasma*, or "flesh," is made of clay (*Ibid.*, V. 6.1). Neither Irenaeus nor Paul uses "flesh," ordinarily, in the Old Testament sense of "human nature" as contrasted with the divine (e.g., Isa. 40:6; Joel 2:28; Matt. 16:17). Whether or not we can achieve a perfect translation is a question; but certainly the RSV has turned a flood of light upon Paul's letters, and upon his thought, which was on the whole consistent but not systematic—he was no medieval Schoolman or modern philosopher of religion.

An example of forcing translation to serve the ends of private views is the astrological version of Job 38:31, "Who can withstand the sweet influences of the Pleiades?" Another is the rendering of the Song of Solomon 1:5 ("I am black but comely, O ye daughters of Jerusalem") in the new South African version—in the land of *apartheid!*—"I am comely, and burnt brown by the sun." Alterations of the text or translation for dogmatic reasons are also apparent, even in some of the most ancient manuscripts. For example, in Matt. 1:16 the Old Syriac and the Old Latin have the phrase, "to whom was betrothed the virgin Mary," instead of "the husband of Mary." And in 1:25, instead of "knew her not," Tatian and the Curetonian Syriac have "lived holily with her," while the Old Latin Codex Bobbiensis (*k*) and the Sinaitic Syriac leave out the sentence altogether and read: "he took his wife, and she bore a son"—the Sinaitic Syriac even reads "bore him a son."

But translation may also be biased on the modern scientific side, as in Luke 1:34, where Mary says to Gabriel at the Annunciation, "How can this be, since I have no husband?" Here the traditional version is definitely superior. "How shall this be, seeing I know not a man?" This agrees with St. Luke's Greek, *pōs estai touto*, "How is this to be?" The reference is to the divine nature and career of her son, who will be both the Son of David and the Son of the Most High, and who will be born to her after her marriage to Joseph, who is a scion of the House of David (vs.27)—this is the whole presupposition of the story, and the words "seeing I know not a man" or "since I have no husband" must have been added later, when the text in Luke came under the influence of the story of the Messiah's birth in Matt. 1:18-25 (see p. 151). It is like the gloss in Luke 3:23 ("as was supposed"), which likewise reflects the influence of Matthew's Infancy Narrative and Genealogy. The translation, "How *can* this be," reflects only the modern scientific problem of the Virgin Birth, not the ethos of the Lucan idyll, which did not question the possibility but only the meaning or the mode of the divine overshadowing and the consequent supernatural nature and destiny of Mary's Child.

There are also special problems connected with the obscure, ambiguous, or uncertain meaning of words. For example, the words of the Risen Lord to Mary of Magdala in John 20:17, where the KJV has "touch me not," as if the condition of his risen body justified ancient Gnostics or modern spiritualists or theosophists in their views; and where a recent translator, E. V. Rieu, has "Do not be alarmed" (*mē ptou* for *mē aptou mou*), which scarcely fits the context, and where the conjectured Greek might perhaps be translated equally well, "Do not distract me" or "excite me" or even "frighten me"; and where the RSV reads "Do not hold me," i.e., restrain me or cling to me, thus preventing Jesus' "return to the Father," which has been the theme of the whole latter half of John's gospel (see 13:1, 33; 14:2, etc.). This last translation fits the context, and the thought of the Johannine gospel as a whole, and the others do not.

Or take the "swaddling clothes" of Luke 2:7, 12 in the KJV. But there are no such clothes, and never were. Both the RV and RSV have "swaddling cloths," which is a compromise. The best English translation is the one in the old hymn, "While shepherds watched their flocks by night" (Nahum Tate, 1652-1715), where the heavenly Babe is "all meanly wrapped in swathing bands." Until recent times, and even now in some regions, newborn infants are wrapped tightly in strips of cloth—not "swaddled" but "swathed," as in Della Robbia's famous *Bambino*.

Other renderings depend upon a conjectural punctuation: there was none, in ancient manuscripts, and words were simply run together, like this:

PILATESAIDTOHIMSOYOUAREAKINGJESUS
ANSWEREDYOUSAYTHATIAMAKING (John 18:37).

This can be taken either as an affirmation or a question; and either as a simple, honest question or as an ironical, contemptuous one. Obviously, the context requires it to be taken as a question. E. V. Rieu paraphrases by amplifying: "So you are a king after all?"—though the Greek justifies this. It is almost: "You are not *really* a king, are you?" But the traditional form of the question is better. Pilate is not trying to convince Jesus, but to engage in the bantering dialogue some lawyers—and even some judges—indulge in. It has often been remarked that John's dramatic "Trial Before Pilate" is a bit of Euripidean dialogue on the Stoic theme of "True Kingship."

Another example is the obscure meaning of the words, "You have said so," in Mark 15:2 and parallels. Was Jesus answering affirmatively, "*Yes*, it is as you say"; or non-committally, "That is what *you* say"; or evasively, "*You* say it!"; or acquiescently, "*You* have said it!"; or even with a

Socratic question, "Would *you* say so?" This problem has been dealt with by editors of the Greek text, translators, and commentators for a long time.[8]

Another example is found in Mark 14:41, "Are you still sleeping and taking your rest? It is enough; the hour has come; the Son of man is betrayed into the hands of sinners." Here the traditional version is impossible: "Sleep on now, and take your rest; it is enough, the hour is come . . ." Still another is John 14:1f., "Let not your hearts be troubled; believe in God, believe also in me. In my Father's house are many rooms; if it were not so, would I have told you that I go to prepare a place for you?" A glance at the King James Version—or the Greek—will show the superiority of the modern rendering.

Another very important verse gives the words of the centurion in charge of the crucifixion (Mark 15:39): "And when the centurion, who stood facing him, saw that he thus [cried out and] breathed his last, he said 'Truly this man was a Son of God' "—*or*, "the Son of God"; *or*, "a son of God," using a lower case *s* for son. There were no distinctions between upper and lower case letters in the most ancient manuscripts; all were written in capitals. The question is, What did Mark intend? The centurion was certainly a pagan, who possibly became a Christian later on—Mark knew several persons, some of them probably members of the church in Rome, whom he does not identify (see 14:9; 15:21); a pagan centurion convinced of the innocence and virtue of Jesus (so Luke understands his words: see Luke

[8] See, e.g., Erich Klostermann in the *Handbuch zum Neuen Testament*, Tübingen, Mohr, 2d ed., 1926, p. 177; and my note in *The Interpreter's Bible*, Vol. VII, 1951, p. 894.

23:47) would certainly use the title in the pagan sense, "a son of a god," i.e., a divine hero, like Hercules, Aesculapius, the Dioscuri—sons of gods who lived as "helpers" of mankind and sometimes, like Hercules, died heroic deaths. That out of this admiring tribute grew a genuine faith in the Son of God, like that of the Gentile Christian Church in Mark's time, is not in the least improbable. And in any event, whether the centurion became a Christian or not, Mark would probably understand—and cite—his testimony to *the* Son of God. Mark's Christology from the beginning was a "Son of God" Christology: the omission of the divine title in some manuscripts of Chapter 1:1 is far easier to explain than its insertion in others.[9] The title of his book— ancient titles were often only the opening words of books— reads, "The beginning of the gospel of [i.e., *about*] Jesus Christ, the Son of God." Repeatedly, Jesus is recognized as the Son of God, even by the wicked spirits (5:7), and here (15:39), at the climax of the Passion Narrative and indeed of the whole gospel, a pagan officer recognizes him as the Son of God. Probability favors the translation, "the Son of God."

Another problem is the sense in which Jesus was to "go before" his disciples to Galilee, after the Resurrection (Mark 14:28; 16:7). In spite of modern theories that Jesus expected to march back to Galilee at the head of his victorious band of followers and there await the establishment of the Kingdom of God in power (Mark 9:1) when Galilee, not Judea or Jerusalem, should become the center of the divine reign on earth, it seems far more probable that the sense is

[9] See my book, *The Gospels, Their Origin and Their Growth,* p. 87; and the Introduction to Mark in *The Interpreter's Bible,* Vol. VII.

temporal: he will precede them, and arrive there in advance of their return. As in the sad Scottish song "Loch Lomond,"

> O, ye'll tak' the high road
> And I'll tak' the low road,
> But I'll be in Scotland afore ye,

so here; only, Jesus was taking the *high* road: death, victory over death, resurrection, and the inauguration of the divine reign, not politically but spiritually. This is how Matthew interprets the words (Matt. 28:7, 10, 16-20), I think rightly. Luke omits the words, for he thinks the church was established in Jerusalem and spread over the world from that center (see Acts 1:4-14). John does not have these words; but John conflates two traditions: the resurrection in Jerusalem, in Chapter 20, and the return to Galilee and commission of the Apostles in the Appendix, Chapter 21.

There are many other passages where the language used, or the state of the text, or the possibility of an early gloss makes the translation difficult. The fact that the works of all ancient authors are under the same handicap, and that their translators are sometimes uncertain of their meaning (even Plato's sublime *Phaedo* has passages of this nature) must moderate our surprise or concern that obscurities survive in the Bible. The sound rule for the translator must be, in all such cases, "When in doubt, be literal." (It would be an advantage if more biblical expositors and translators had experience with classical texts, and also paid more attention to the textual apparatus in modern editions!) Take Matt. 5:22 for example. Does "without cause" belong in the text? —it is only one short four-letter word in Greek, *eikē*. There is a story, probably apocryphal, that the irascible King

James remarked, when he first read the new version which he had authorized, " 'Without a cause'—what a blessed provision!" Who was ever angry "without cause"? It is everybody's "alibi," and a very poor one! Surely the word *eikē* is some early copyist's addition.

Or take Romans 5:1, "Therefore, since we are justified by faith, we have peace with God through our Lord Jesus Christ." "We have peace"—*echomen;* but some modern translators and interpreters prefer the manuscripts (good ones!) which read *echōmen*, "let us have peace": the difference between the two words, one the finite present tense, the other the hortatory subjunctive, is only that one has a short *o* (omicron), the other a long *ō* (omega). In ancient manuscripts the latter was often written like the former, with a bar beneath it (rather than above it, as in modern transliteration). This bar often faded, or grew faint for other reasons; and sometimes it was added by copyists who thought the sense required its addition. Such copyists were not "tampering with Scripture," but were making the same kind of corrections that many of us do in misspelled words, as we read our new books: obviously, we think, the author intended the meaning we take to be the true one. In his fascinating book, *What Is the Best New Testament?* Ernest Colwell has a capital illustration: who would question the propriety of correcting a dictionary definition that read, "A horse is an animal with five legs"? Of course, it should read *four!*—But what did Paul write? Hardly "let us"; for Paul was a Jew, and a first-century Christian, and a theist who believed in the absolute sovereignty of God. He would never suggest that we bad human beings should lift our faces to the God who is "of purer eyes than to behold [i.e., to tolerate] iniquity" and say, "Let us have peace." Between man and man, between nations, yes; as in the words of General Ulysses Grant, inscribed on his tomb in New York City, words that brought the terrible, inexcusable War between the States to an end. But not between men and God. For peace with God, it is God who must—and does—take the initiative: this is written all over Paul's teaching, as it is all over the Bible, Old Testament and New. Paul wrote as he believed, *ex animo*, with every fibre of his being: "Since we are justified by faith [by God's act, conditional only upon our faith, not our full performance of righteous works in advance of justification], we *have* peace with God through our Lord Jesus Christ." This is the key to the central citadel of all Paul's religious teaching and theology.

I have reserved to the end a translation which has puzzled some persons, but has caused many to rejoice. Almost the first action of the Revised Standard Version Committee was to abandon the transliteration "Jehovah" and go back to the older English Bible tradition, "the Lord," spelled LORD, with two-size capitals. Though introduced by Tyndale, the word "Jehovah" is a hybrid, the consonants of the ancient Hebrew word for God YHWH, which by about 200 B.C. was no longer pronounced (out of reverence), plus the vowels of the word *Adonai* ("my Lord") which was substituted for it in the public reading of the Bible in the synagogue. No ancient Jew tried to pronounce "Yahowah," but understood that he was to read "the Lord" when he came to the sacred tetragrammaton. This usage was followed by the ancient translators, in both the Septuagint (*Kyrios*, Lord) and the Vulgate (*Dominus*). The word "Jehovah" is a late medieval attempt to make a Christian word of the unpronounceable hybrid. As explained in the Preface to the Revised Standard Version,

> (1) The word "Jehovah" does not accurately represent any form of the Name ever used in Hebrew; and (2) the use of any proper name for the one and only God, as though there were other gods from whom he had to be distinguished, was discontinued in Judaism before the Christian era and is entirely inappropriate for the universal faith of the Christian Church.

It is not surprising that the churches in America should be interested in Bible revision, or should have produced the Revised Standard Version, the latest revision in the long line beginning with Tyndale, Coverdale, Matthews, and continuing with the Great Bible, the Geneva Bible, the Rheims New Testament, the Bishops' Bible, the King James Bible, the Revised Version. Bible translation is in our blood. The first book to be printed in New England was *The Psalms in Metre*, in 1640. And the equipment in scholarship was not lacking. The schoolmaster of the Jamestown Settlement, in Virginia, occupied his leisure in translating Ovid.

Certainly still more translations and revisions will be called for: we cannot foresee, we can only guess, the direction in which modern English is moving and will continue to move. Nor can we foresee the direction in which biblical scholarship will advance—though advance it certainly will, as "time marches on," as more old manuscripts are discovered, and as we come to understand ancient Hebrew, Aramaic, and Greek even better. One thing at least we might do, right away: bring the translations of Holy Scripture that appear in the

Prayer Book into greater accord with the best modern scholarship. Take the Psalms, which are still in Coverdale's version. Some passages are meaningless—like Psalm 2:12, "Kiss the Son, lest he be angry, and so ye perish from the right way, if his wrath be kindled, yea but a little." What a waste and loss of people's devotion, to read such solemn nonsense at divine worship! Or Psalm 6:6, "Every night wash I my bed"—the comma after "bed" makes the verse ridiculous. Or Psalm 9:15, "The heathen are sunk down," where it is the *nations*, resorting to violence (as in Psalm 2); "heathen" is not a very good word today. In our modern international "one world" the religious man's prayer may still be voiced in the words of the psalmist:

> Arise, O Lord! Let not man prevail;
>   let the nations be judged before thee!
> Put them in fear, O Lord!
>   Let the nations know that they are but men!
>   (Psalm 9:19-20)

Translated correctly, in modern idiom but with complete accuracy and faithfulness to the original, the Psalms—and also the Prophets—take on a vigor and a relevance one would never suspect from the traditional versions. These examples are a few from the first ten Psalms. One could go through the Psalter and find dozens of passages where slight changes might be made, still keeping the rhythm and beauty of Coverdale's style, but releasing more of the power and triumphant faith of the ancient writers. The same is true of the Epistles and Gospels. There are a few dozen passages which cry out for revision—not for a radical rewriting, but only the substitution of better diction, more accurate, more understandable. If we were to do this, our Prayer Book would glow with added meaning for us all, for priests and people, for old and young, for children and the aged, all of us together. This meaning lies just under the surface, and a slight—a very slight—polishing would bring it out once more, as once it came out in Jerome's three Psalters, and again in Coverdale's, and in the King James.

The Bible is the church's Book. This has been so from the beginning. Its place is on the lectern—open, for all to read. It is the textbook of religion, teaching us "the way of God in truth." In order to fulfill its purpose, it must continue to be "understood by the people," and speak directly and intimately to their inmost hearts, to their conscience and their hope, to their aspiration toward God and his goodness, to their practice of faith and love, to their deepest ties with others and their most secret convictions about the meaning of life, the purpose of human existence, both of communities and of individuals. Chiefly, the Bible is the book used in worship—and for this purpose it has been translated, revised, and retranslated countless times, from the very beginning, so that it may continue to speak "the language of men." It is used wherever prayer is offered. For we are bidden to "pray with the spirit," and to "pray with the mind also" (1 Cor. 14:15). We are all one fellowship, sharers in a common faith, a common purpose, a common task; we are devoted to a common Lord, to whom we offer our common worship. In the words of John Ellerton's beloved hymn,

We thank thee that thy Church, unsleeping
   While earth rolls onward into light,
Through all the world her watch is keeping,
   And rests not now by day or night.

As o'er each continent and island
   The dawn leads on another day,
The voice of prayer is never silent,
   Nor dies the strain of praise away.

So be it, Lord; thy throne shall never,
   Like earth's proud empires, pass away;
Thy kingdom stands, and grows for ever,
   Till all thy creatures own thy sway.

At the heart of this unending, world-wide worship is the
Bible, which contains God's message to all mankind.

FOR

FURTHER

READING

Books of unusual importance, especially for the beginner, are marked with an asterisk.

* *The Authorized Version of the Bible* (reprinted from the first edition, 1611). Oxford University Press, 1911.

Berger, Samuel. *Histoire de la Vulgate* pendant les premiers siecles du moyen age. Paris, 1893. Photographic reprint, New York, 1959.

Bewer, J. A. *The Literature of the Old Testament.* New York: Columbia University Press, new ed., 1933.

Bookman's Year Book, 1955 (=Antiquarian Bookman Annual) ; on Gutenberg Bibles today.

* Bridges, Ronald, and Weigle, Luther. *The Bible Word Book.* New York: Nelson, 1960.

* Burrows, Millar. *The Dead Sea Scrolls.* New York: Viking Press, 1956.

———. *More Light on the Dead Sea Scrolls.* New York: Viking Press, 1959.

Charles, R. H. *The Apocrypha and Pseudepigrapha of the Old Testament.* Oxford University Press, two vols., 1913.

The Codex Sinaiticus. The Codex Alexandrinus. London: The British Museum, 1955.

* Colwell, E. C. *The Study of the Bible.* University of Chicago Press, 1937.

——. *What Is the Best New Testament?* University of Chicago Press, 1952.

The Complete Concordance of the Revised Standard Version of the Bible. Thomas Nelson & Sons, 1957.

Daiches, David. *The King James Version of the English Bible.* University of Chicago Press, 1941.

Deanesly, Margaret. *The Lollard Bible and Other Medieval Biblical Versions.* Cambridge University Press, 1920.

——. *The Significance of the Lollard Bible.* London University Press, 1951.

* Dodd, C. H. *The Bible and the Greeks.* London: Hodder & Stoughton, 1935.

Driver, G. R. *The Hebrew Scrolls.* Oxford University Press, 1951.

Field, Frederick. *Notes on the Translation of the New Testament.* Cambridge University Press, 1899.

Filson, F. V. *Which Books Belong in the Bible?* Philadelphia: Westminster Press, 1957.

Fragments of an Unknown Gospel, and Other Early Papyri. London: British Museum, 1935.

Goodspeed, E. J. *Introduction to the New Testament.* University of Chicago Press, 1937.

——. *The Story of the Apocrypha.* University of Chicago Press, 1939.

* ———. *Problems of New Testament Translation.* University of Chicago Press, 1945.

* Goodspeed, E. J. (ed.) *The Translators to the Reader* (the Preface to the King James Version). University of Chicago Press, 1935.

Grant, F. C. Article "Exegesis," in *Encyclopedia Americana*, Vol. X, pp. 628-636.

———. Articles "Tyndale" (Vol. XXVII, pp. 234f.) and "Wycliffe" (Vol. XXIX, pp. 580f.).

———. *How to Read the Bible.* New York: Morehouse-Gorham, 1956; Edinburgh: Nelson, 1959.

———. *The Gospels, Their Origin and Their Growth.* New York: Harper & Bros., 1956; London: Faber & Faber, 1958.

———. *Ancient Judaism and the New Testament.* New York: Macmillan, 1959; Edinburgh: Oliver & Boyd, 1960.

Grant, F. C. (ed.) Articles on the Bible, including text and versions of Old and New Testaments, in *Encyclopedia Americana*, new edition, Vol. III, pp. 612-671f.

* Grant, Robert M. *The Bible in the Church.* New York: Macmillan, 1948; rev. ed., 1954.

———. *The Letter and the Spirit.* London: S.P.C.K., 1957.

Gray, G. B. *The Forms of Hebrew Poetry.* London: Hodder and Stoughton, 1915.

Greenslade, S. L. *The Work of William Tyndale.* London: Blackie & Son, 1938.

Harnack, Adolf. *Bible Reading in the Early Church.* London: Williams & Norgate, 1912.

Harper's Bible Dictionary. New York: Harper & Bros., 1952; new ed. 1955.

Hastings' *Dictionary of the Bible* (one vol.). New York:

Scribners; Edinburgh: Clark, 1909. New edition in preparation.

* Herklots, H. G. G. *How Our Bible Came to Us*. Oxford University Press, 1954; revised ed. in the "Pelican" series, Penguin Books, 1959.

Hetzenauer, M. *Biblia Sacra Vulgatae Editionis*. Innsbruck, 1906 and later.

Hunter, A. M. *Interpreting the New Testament, 1900-1950*. London: S.C.M., 1952.

Hutson, H. H., and Willoughby, H. R. *The Ignored Taverner Bible of 1539*. University of Chicago Press, 1939.

——. *Decisive Data on Thomas Matthew* [Bible] *Problems*. University of Chicago Press, 1938.

* *The Interpreter's Bible* (a commentary). Nashville: Abingdon Press; Edinburgh: Nelson, 1951-1957, 12 vols.

* James, M. R. *The Apocryphal New Testament*. Oxford University Press, 1924.

* Kahle, Paul E. *The Cairo Geniza*. Oxford: Blackwell, new ed., 1959.

* Kenyon, Frederic. *Our Bible and the Ancient Manuscripts*. New ed. by A. W. Adams. London: Eyre & Spottiswood, 1958.

——. *The Text of the Greek Bible*. New York: Scribners; London: Duckworth, new ed., 1949.

——. *Recent Developments in the Textual Criticism of the Greek Bible*. London: British Academy, 1933.

* ——. *The Story of the Bible*. London: John Murray, Ltd., 1936.

Knox, Ronald. *Trials of a Translator*. New York: Sheed

& Ward, 1949; (English title, *On Englishing the Bible*. London: Burns Oates, 1949).

* Lake, Kirsopp. *The Text of the New Testament*. London: Rivingtons, 7th ed., 1928.

Lightfoot, J. B. *On a Fresh Revision of the English New Testament*. London, 1871.

* Lund, Nils. *Chiasmus in the New Testament*. Chapel Hill: University of North Carolina Press, 1942.

* Malden, R. H. *The Apocrypha*. New York: Oxford University Press, 1936.

Manson, T. W. *The Sayings of Jesus*. London: S.C.M., 1949.

Manson, T. W. (ed.) *A Companion to the Bible*. New York: Scribners, 1939.

MacGregor, Geddes. *The Bible in the Making*. New York: Lippincott, 1959.

May, H. G. *Our English Bible in the Making*. Philadelphia: Westminster, 1952.

* Metzger, B. M. *An Introduction to the Apocrypha*. Oxford University Press, 1957.

Moffatt, James. *Introduction to the Literature of the New Testament*. New York: Scribners, new ed., 1911.

* Mohrmann, Christine. *Liturgical Latin, Its Origin and Character*. Washington: Catholic University of America, 1957; London: Burns Oates, 1959.

Moore, E. C. *The New Testament in the Christian Church*. New York: Macmillan, 1904.

Moule, C. F. D. *The Language of the New Testament*. Cambridge University Press, 1952.

Mozley, J. F. *Coverdale and His Bibles*. London: Lutterworth Press, 1953.

——. *William Tyndale*. London: Lutterworth Press, 1937.

Neil, William (ed.). *The Bible Companion*. London: Skeffington; New York: McGraw-Hill, 1960.

Nestle, Eberhard. Article "Septuagint" in Hastings' *Dictionary of the Bible*, Vol. IV, pp. 437-454. Edinburgh: Clark; New York: Scribners, 1902.

Nestle, Eberhard. *Einführung in das Neue Testament*. New ed. rev. by Ernst von Dobschütz. Göttingen: Vandenhoeck und Ruprecht, 1923.

——. *Novum Testamentum Graece*. Stuttgart: Württemberg Bible Society, 23rd ed., 1957. Now ed. by Erwin Nestle. See the very useful Introduction, in four languages.

* *The New Gospel Fragments*. London: British Museum, 1955.

New Standard Bible Dictionary. New York: Funk & Wagnalls, new ed., 1936.

* North, Eric (ed.). *The Book of a Thousand Tongues*. New York: American Bible Society, 1938.

Pfeiffer, Robert H. *Introduction to the Old Testament*. New York: Harper & Bros., 1938.

——. *History of New Testament Times, with Introduction to the Apocrypha*. New York: Harper & Bros., 1954.

Pollard, Alfred W. *Records of the English Bible*. New York: Oxford University Press, 1911. The final document is the famous Preface of the King James Version, *The Translators to the Reader*.

* Price, Ira M. *The Ancestry of Our English Bible*. Revised by W. M. Irwin and Allen Wikgren. New York: Harper & Bros., 1949.

* *The Revised Standard Version of the Bible*. New York:

Nelson; Edinburgh: Nelson; *New Testament*, 1946; *Old Testament*, 1952; *Apocrypha*, 1957. Separately or in combination, many editions.

Roberts, B. J. *The Old Testament Text and Versions*. Cardiff: University of Wales, 1951.

* Robinson, H. W. *The Bible in Its Ancient and English Versions*. Oxford University Press, 1940; revised ed., ill., 1954.

Robinson, T. H. *The Poetry of the Old Testament*. London: Duckworth, 1947.

Rowley, H. H. *The Relevance of the Bible*. London: James Clarke, 1942.

——. *The Rediscovery of the Old Testament*. London: James Clarke, 1946.

——. *The Dead Sea Scrolls and the New Testament*. London: S.P.C.K., 1957.

—— (ed.). *The Old Testament and Modern Study*. Oxford University Press, 1951.

Schubert, Kurt. *The Dead Sea Community*. New York: Harper, 1959.

Schwarz, W. *Principles and Problems of Biblical Translation:* Some Reformation Controversies and Their Background. Cambridge University Press, 1955.

Scott, E. F. *The Literature of the New Testament*. New York: Columbia University Press, 1932.

Scrivener, F. H. A. *The Authorized Edition of the English Bible 1611*. Cambridge University Press, 1884.

Smalley, Beryl. *The Study of the Bible in the Middle Ages*. Oxford University Press, 1941.

Swaim, J. Carter. *Right and Wrong Ways to Use the Bible*. Philadelphia: Westminster Press, 1953.

———. *Do You Understand the Bible?* Philadelphia: West-minster Press, 1954.

Swete, H. B. *An Introduction to the Old Testament in Greek.* Cambridge University Press, 1900.

* Thackeray, H. St. J. *The Letter of Aristeas.* London: S.P.C.K., 1917.

* Throckmorton, B. H. *Gospel Parallels.* New York: Nelson; Edinburgh: Nelson, 1949; new ed., 1957. A "Synopsis" or "Harmony" of the Synoptic Gospels in parallel columns, based on the arrangement and numbering of A. Huck's famous *Synopse der drei ersten Evangelien* (in Greek), but using the RSV text.

Trench, R. C. *On the Authorized Version of the New Testament.* London, new ed., reprinted 1959.

Vogels, H. J. *Handbuch der Textkritik des Neuen Testaments.* Bonn: Hanstein, 1955, 2nd ed.

* Wallis, N. H. (ed.). *Tyndale's New Testament.* Cambridge University Press, 1938. (Reprint of the 1534 edition.)

* Weigle, L. A. (ed.). *An Introduction to the Revised Standard Version of the New Testament.* New York: Nelson, 1946.

* Weigle, L. A. (ed.). *An Introduction to the Revised Standard Version of the Old Testament.* New York: Nelson, 1952.

* ———. *The Bible Word Book.* New York: Nelson, 1960.

———. *Bible Words That Have Changed in Meaning.* New York: Nelson, 1955. (A list of 857 words used in the King James Version, with biblical references for each.)

———. *The English New Testament from Tyndale to the Revised Standard Version.* New York: Nelson, 1949.

Westcott, B. F. *A General View of the History of the English Bible*. London: Macmillan, 1868, and later.

——. *Some Lessons of the Revised Version of the New Testament*. London, 4th ed., 1903.

Willoughby, Edwin E. *The Making of the King James Bible*. Los Angeles, privately printed, 1956.

* Willoughby, H. R. *The Coverdale Psalter and the Quatrocentenary of the Printed English Bible*, with a Facsimile Reproduction of the Psalter. Chicago: Caxton Club, 1935.

——. *The First Authorized English Bible and the Cranmer Preface*. University of Chicago Press, 1942.

Workman, H. B. *John Wycliffe: A Study of the English Medieval Church*. Oxford University Press, 1926.

Wright, W. A. *The Bible Word Book*. London, second ed. 1884.

* Würthwein, E. *The Text of the Old Testament*. Oxford: B. Blackwell, 1957.

INDEX

I. Persons

Adams, A. W., 101
Aelfric, Abbot, 52
Albright, William F.,
108
Alfred, King, 51
Allan, D. J., 132
Allen, Wm. H., 131
Ammonius of Alexan-
dria, 38
Anderson, Charles, 76
Anderson, G. W., 114
Andrewes, Lancelot, 48
Aquila, 24, 37, 93
Aristeas, 20
Armagh, Abp. of, 114
Arnold, Matthew, 131
Arundel, Archbishop, 59
Augustine, 22, 31, 45,
48, 72, 94, 118, 145
Augustine of Canter-
bury, 50
Auvray, P., 100

Bacon, Francis, 47
Barker, Robert, 76
Barry, Alfred, 144
Baxter, William, 127
Bede, the Venerable, 50
Béguin, Albert, 101
Benoit, P., 100
Bensly, Robert L., 124
Bewer, Julius A., 107
Bèze, Theodore de, 88
Black, Matthew, 114
Boleyn, Anne, 63

Bois, John, 77
Bover, J. M., 117
Bowie, Walter Russell,
107
Brockington, L. H., 113
Browning, Robert, 87
Burnet, John, 124, 132
Burrows, Millar, 107f.

Cadbury, Henry J.,
107f.
Cadman, W. H., 113
Caedmon, 50
Calvin, John, 69
Camerarius, Joachim,
125
Campbell, J. Y., 113
Carrouges, Michel, 100
Cerfaux, L., 100
Chaucer, Geoffrey, 55
Challoner, Richard, 70,
100
Charles I, 27
Charles, R. H., 110
Chrysostom, 81
Clement of Alexandria,
131
Collins, William, 95
Colwell, Ernest, 159
Constantine, 31
Coverdale, Miles, 63,
65f.
Craig, Clarence T., 108
Craigie, William, 57

Cranmer, Archbishop,
65, 68
Cromwell, Thomas, 67
Cureton, William, 35
Cuthbert, 50
Cyprian of Carthage,
35
Cyril Lucar, 27

Dahl, George, 107
Dale, H. E., 132
Damasus, Pope, 36, 38
Dante, 48
Della Robbia, 155
Dodd, C. H., 112
Donne, John, 48
Driver, G. R., 113
Duncan, G. S., 113

Edward VI, 70
Elizabeth I, 72
Ellerton, John, 163
Emmerson, Margaret
van, 63
Erasmus, Desiderius,
62, 68, 77, 88, 116
Eusebius, 26, 38
Eustochium, 39
Ewes, Symonds d', 121
Ezra, 6, 7ff.

Feild, John, 77
Filson, Floyd V., 108,
110
Fox, Adam, 113

II. Subjects

III. Texts